Why I Turned Right ⫸→

★

Leading Baby Boom
Conservatives Chronicle Their
Political Journeys

★

Edited and with an Introduction by

Mary Eberstadt

THRESHOLD
EDITIONS

New York   London   Toronto   Sydney

THRESHOLD EDITIONS
A Division of Simon & Schuster, Inc.
1230 Avenue of the Americas
New York, NY 10020

First Threshold Editions trade paperback edition October 2008

THRESHOLD EDITIONS and colophon are trademarks of Simon & Schuster, Inc.

For information about special discounts for bulk purchases,
please contact Simon & Schuster Special Sales at
1-800-456-6798 or business@simonandschuster.com.

Designed by William Ruoto

Manufactured in the United States of America

10 9 8 7 6 5 4 3 2 1

Library of Congress Cataloging-in-Publication Data

ISBN-13: 978-1-4165-2855-5
ISBN-10:   1-4165-2855-5
ISBN-13: 978-1-4165-2856-2 (pbk)
ISBN-10:   1-4165-2856-3 (pbk)

CONTENTS

Contents

INTRODUCTION
by Mary Eberstadt

This book is a unique attempt to answer a question that continues to confound many observers both American and otherwise: *Why conservatism?* It does so not through shrill polemic or high-decibel rage, but rather in the most practical and informative way possible: via the unfiltered voices of a dozen leading authors and editors of the contemporary right, including some of the best-known and most influential in the country. Peter Berkowitz, David Brooks, Joseph Bottum, Danielle Crittenden, Dinesh D'Souza, Stanley Kurtz, Tod Lindberg, Rich Lowry, Heather Mac Donald, P. J. O'Rourke, Sally Satel, and Richard Starr all tell their stories here. They explain how they came to reside on the conservative side of America's red-blue divide—in some cases, to their own surprise.

The utility of such a volume in this particular political moment is evident. For one thing, following 9/11, two terms of George W. Bush, Democratic victories in fall 2006, and controversial wars in Afghanistan and Iraq, the mood on the right itself is one of introspection and soul-searching. For another, and despite significant disenchantment among some, the overall conservative realignment of the United States is still one of the biggest political stories of the past quarter century. It remains so with or without Bush in the White House, whether or not the American military continues its mission in Iraq, and regardless of who holds the next majority in Congress or on the Supreme Court. The November 2006 elections—in which Democrats roundly prevailed by promising for the first time since Bill Clinton to govern from the center, and a handful of right-leaning Democratic candidates defeated Republicans unaccustomed to attack from that wing—clinch the point about our political sea change. Whatever the particular fortunes of the Republican Party one year, two years, or five years hence, the United States as a whole has plainly moved right.

Yet even though many more Americans are now likely to self-identify as "conservative" rather than "liberal," the reasons for that transformation remain questions of enduring public wonder and scrutiny—not least from Cambridge to San Francisco and everywhere blue in between. How *did* a movement that appeared sidelined and embattled only a generation ago come to exert such influence that even the Democratic Party now tacks starboard? What accounts for the unprecedented growth and reach of right-leaning think tanks, magazines, television, and radio? What, in short, has been *happening* out there such that so many Americans are now comfortable with the conservative label, or, conversely, so averse to contemporary liberalism?

During the last several years, any number of high-profile attempts to answer those questions have circulated from all political directions. Homegrown progressives have gone puzzling over their fellow citizens (Thomas Frank's *What's the Matter with Kansas?*, Jim Wallis's *God's Politics: Why the Right Gets It Wrong and the Left Doesn't Get It*), Englishmen have gone puzzling over Yanks (John Micklethwait and Adrian Wooldridge, *The Right Nation*), rank-breakers of all kinds have gone puzzling over everything from fellow conservatives to their former selves (Kevin Phillips, *American Theocracy*, Francis Fukuyama, *America at the Crossroads*, Bruce Bartlett, *Impostor*). We have even seen one soi-disant latter-day Tocqueville (Bernard-Henri Lévy, *American Vertigo*) traverse the country and sally through its social classes from high to low, in part to divine the same political mystery. And still the question for many people—especially, though not only, liberals—remains: *How can so many supposedly rational fellow citizens out there believe all that backward reactionary stuff?*

That is exactly what our contributors, all leading lights in one way or another in the intellectual firmament of the current right, wish to explain here.

≫→

That such a book might make for interesting reading was a thought kindled in me some months back during a conversation with P. J. O'Rourke about the striking number of political conversion stories we each knew. We had in mind not the eminent converts of the preceding generation, many of whom had moved from youthful socialism through the liberalism of their time and on into neoconservatism—Irving Kristol, Norman Podhoretz, and the rest—but rather, the so-far-untold tales from those who came next. These "younger" writers like us, now roughly in middle age, had attended college in the postliberationist 1970s and 1980s, when liberal-left thinking was not the dominant game on campus, but in many places the only one. What had happened, we wondered, to push this new generation away from the "default" position embraced by so many of our campus peers?

This book is the result of pursuing that question, which I was particularly curious to see through for two reasons—first, because the fact that I had also "traveled" in some political sense gave me a natural interest in it; second, because my past and present associations as editor or author at various journals and magazines (*The Public Interest, The National Interest,* the *Weekly Standard, Policy Review, First Things*) had given me some inkling already of how many more such stories might be out there.

Like me, the authors of the pages ahead know the right not only from the outside in, but also from the inside out. All represent in one form or another the venues through which many ideas are made and disseminated—journals including *National Review, City Journal, Commentary,* and those others named above; think tanks, including the Hoover Institution, the American Enterprise Institute, and the Manhattan Institute; "alternative" media like Fox News, nation-alreview.com, and many other blogs and sites followed by conservatives. Thus, these contributors represent in minia-ture the generation now peopling the right-leaning think tanks and airwaves and internet and book and magazine publishing—in a word, some of the human nuts and bolts of what Hillary Clinton once disparaged as the "vast right-wing conspiracy."

Of course "conservatism" in America is no monolith, and these pages reflect that reality, too. Their criterion for what is right is simply the obvious one: It's what those on the other side call you whenever you put your head up and they feel like taking a shot. As Irving Kristol observed two decades ago in *Reflections of a Neoconservative:*

> The key ideological terms of modern political
> debate have all been either invented or popularized by
> the Left—"liberal," "conservative," and "reactionary,"
> "socialist" and "capitalist," "Left" and "Right"
> themselves—so that it is extremely difficult for
> those on the non-Left to come up with an adequate
> self-definition. . . . The sensible course, therefore, is to
> take your label, claim it as your own, and run with it.

And so we will do here. The practical fact is that if you are (for example) a fellow at the Hoover Institution, and write for the likes of *Policy Review* or any other journal that is not the *New Yorker* or the *Nation,* and publish anything at all, ever, that locates you to the right of, say, Michael Moore, then the *New York Times* will call you a "conservative"—an "ultraconservative" if you really annoy them—no matter what fine-tuned harrumphing variations with hyphens you yourself might prefer. "They" see "us" as a united front, and so for purposes of simplicity will we see ourselves here.

Naturally, reality on inspection could show otherwise. About any number of specific ideas—the war in Iraq, immigration, gay marriage, stem cell research—many conservatives, including those ahead, disagree. The perpetual tug of war between libertarianism and social conservatism, for example, runs firmly (if tacitly) between the lines of these pages, as could the tension between "democratism" and "realism" in foreign policy had these same authors been asked to debate the war in Iraq. Even so, one common denominator holds: These are not the only writers of their generation who could pen an essay explaining how they left the "default" position of left/liberalism behind to become something else. For every essay in these pages, any number by other authors with related con-version stories could have taken its place. That's how widespread the flight right has been. And that, in a way, is precisely the point of this book.

>>→

So what *did* happen to make the right the intellectual and political residence of these particular writers? Though their nuances and experiences differ, the tales told here do play variations on distinct themes.

For some, the answer begins in foreign policy—or rather, in the excruciating national humiliation that they associate with the years 1976–80. "Jimmy Carter made me the conservative I am today, as I suspect he did many members of my generation." So summarizes Richard Starr, managing editor of the *Weekly Standard,* and so undoubtedly would many fellow travelers agree. Further specifying "a visceral reaction against the moral chaos and defeatism of the 1970s," Starr makes vivid this perhaps overlooked point about the reaction against the liberalism of that time: Something about a twenty-year-old, especially, does not love being told to suck it up and turn down the heat and blame yourself or America first—and to put up with the hostage crisis because any proposed alternative to defeatism is bound to be worse.

In short, Ronald Reagan's election in 1980, as is widely held, may indeed have been unthinkable without Jimmy Carter, but Carter's influence in one perverse sense may have yet to be measured in full. For in the outcry against what he and his policies stood for, the *American Spectator* and any number of polemical imitators on campuses were born—sharp, critical, and often shockingly funny vessels of the right that would go on to mock and deflate the worst of contemporary liberalism, and to influence and animate conservatism and create new converts, long after Carter and even Reagan himself had exited the scene.

A second factor making intermittent appearances in these journeys is the political fallout of plain old human experience—including experience of some of the human wreckage brought on by the sexual revolution. Several years ago, in his novel *A Man in Full,* Tom Wolfe offered up a twentysomething character named Conrad Helmsley. The product of hippie parents and an adult world running pell-mell away from every convention, Conrad finds himself longing for exactly what the grown-ups have all so willfully abandoned: "He was not even eleven when he first began to entertain the subversive notion that 'bourgeois' might in fact be something he just might want to be when he grew up."

Order, convention, family life, religion, respectability, solidity: For some contributors, just seeing the postliberation scene up close and too personal was enough to cause them to think that Conrad Helmsley might be right—including and perhaps especially those whose own stories owe more to St. Augustine, say, than to Cotton Mather. Explains P. J. O'Rourke:

> I was swept out to Marxist sea by a flood of sex.
> I was trying to impress cute beatnik girls. Then, one
> day, I found myself washed up on the shore of jobs

and responsibilities, and I was a Republican again. . . . Think of me as Michael Oakeshott without the brain.

The flip side of quotidian domestic experience is also cited by several writers: that is, the political effect of becoming a parent. "I became a conservative at 11:59 P.M. on December 4, 1997, the way many people become conservatives," reports O'Rourke again, now from the other side of the fence. "My wife gave birth." "As the parent of an eleven-year-old daughter," Dinesh D'Souza shares, "I am more socially conservative now than I ever have been. In fact, of late I've been thinking that I might need a gun." Further tying political evolution rightward not only to children but also to marriage, Danielle Crittenden writes, "We [modern humans] continue to maintain the illusion that we are entirely self-sufficient creatures whose destiny is fully in our own hands. That illusion doesn't hold up so well when you meet the man whose destiny you wish to share—and shatters entirely when you become responsible for the destinies of new people whom you have given life."

Another factor cited in several essays is the sheer transformative power of conservative ideas—past and present. "[Allan] Bloom framed the issues," writes former ACLU-style liberal Stanley Kurtz, "and in the process changed my life. *The Closing of the American Mind* gave voice to a thousand fugitive thoughts and feelings I'd only half-acknowledged for years." Similarly, Peter Berkowitz: "[Leo] Strauss's reconciliation of the critique of liberalism with the defense of liberal democracy left a lasting impression on me." Several writers share a streak of autodidactism made stronger by exposure via conservative journalism to persuasive, hitherto unknown texts. As Rich Lowry describes the process in his particular case:

> I was led from references in *National Review* to certain books, which led in turn to more books. There were the basics, Barry Goldwater's *The Conscience of a Conservative,* Buckley's *Up from Liberalism,* Russell Kirk's *The Conservative Mind.* But these were just an entrée. James Burnham's accessible polemic *Suicide of the West*—a broad-gauged attack on liberalism, especially its foreign policy—led me to his *The Managerial Elite,* a sophisticated work of sociology, and then on to *The Machiavellians,* a work of philosophy. Before I knew it, I was lounging away summer afternoons on the roof of my parents' back porch trying to follow Burnham's explications of the thought of Robert Michels and Vilfredo Pareto.

There is also the practical fact that some authors served apprenticeships at flagship journals including *The Public Interest, American Spectator, The National Interest,* and other publications of sufficiently high quality that their back issues are still livelier reading than most of what is pub-lished—let alone blogged or posted—today. Tod Lindberg, whose own editorial career has spanned numerous periodi-cals of the right, summarizes the excitement: "It's some-thing entirely different to discover the world of the 'little' magazine, in which brilliant people bandied about ideas with robust incisiveness and great wit. This was news to me—very good news."

If it is true, as many observers have remarked or com-plained depending on disposition, that conservatism has trumped liberalism in generating ideas these last few de-cades, the success of the right's nonconspiratorial apprentice system of the 1980s especially—R. Emmett Tyrell's *American Spectator* in Indiana, Irving Kristol's tiny one-room *Public Interest* office in Manhattan, William F. Buckley's rather larger and also young and boisterous *National Review* quarters—might be one overlooked reason why.

$$\gg\!\!\rightarrow$$

Similarly, and perhaps most dramatically, one other under-acknowledged answer to *"Why conservatism?"* suggests itself repeatedly in the essays of *Why I Turned Right*: academia, or more properly the staggeringly uniform and unforgiving creed of ideological correctness against which almost every one of these writers sooner or later set his face.

In retrospect, that very kind of academy may turn out to be the real cradle of conservatism as we know it—in a purely negative sense, that is. For one thing, and as psychiatrist Sally Satel's essay in particular makes clear, at least some baby boom/gen X writers turned right who might otherwise have stayed in the political middle—because in elite academia from the late 1960s on, there was often no middle to be found. Just how monolithic those places were some twenty years ago—or at least the chic precincts to which eager young generalists might be drawn—can be seen in the pile-on of top-this academic anecdotes.

Heather Mac Donald's account of what deconstruction was perpetrating upon students at Yale during those years offers perhaps the most in-depth case study. With the literary treasures of Western civilization under attack by a host of European-inspired academic insurgents, she writes, "The university had abdicated its educational responsibility, leaving students to their worst instincts. . . . Students rarely heard counterarguments to deconstruction's juvenile nihilism or learned why they would be better off sweating over Latin syntax and Gibbon than Michel Foucault and Julia Kristeva." And Yale was far from alone in tenuring absurdity and ostracizing the sane. Elsewhere, Mac Donald summarizes:

> Cringing administrators replaced the Western
> culture requirement with something suitably

multicultural, and the criterion of excellence in the
selection of academic material was forever abolished.
Every other university, faced with copycat protests by
barely literate teenagers, sacrificed its precious cargo
of masterpieces with equally cowardly alacrity.

At Dartmouth, relates Dinesh D'Souza in one of the
kinds of anecdotes that made the ground-breaking contrarian *Dartmouth Review* a cause célèbre, there was, among other
problems:

> . . . . the radicalism of the feminist professors on
> campus. These women made statements to the effect
> that all males were potential rapists. One professor
> said she could barely walk around the Dartmouth
> campus because the tall tower of Baker Library upset
> her so deeply. To her, the tall buildings at Dartmouth
> were "phallic symbols." Apparently this woman's
> definition of a phallic symbol was anything that was
> longer than it was wide.

That kind of feminism so closely associated with the
liberalism of the time—that "spinsterish fear of the male sex
drive," in Danielle Crittenden's phrase—was naturally off-
putting to some men, but not only to them. As Crittenden
also writes of the then-dominant "difference feminists," "It's
thanks to them that companies were forced to pay out mil-

lions of dollars in legal settlements because somebody made the wrong kind of joke over the water cooler. And it's thanks to them that so many young, confident women were put off by their wince-making brand of feminism." Like the political correctness to which it was aligned, extreme feminism appears to have had a jujitsu effect—summoning by the sheer size and force of its wrongheadedness the very political reaction it sought to prevent.

In fact, so ideologically overboard was the overall American academic scene during the years in which most contributors passed through that one author, formerly apolitical science student Sally Satel, reports political awakening on account of something happening *elsewhere:*

> There was one more formative event for me
> that had nothing whatever to do with me personally:
> the 1993 water buffalo case at the University of
> Pennsylvania. At the center of the incident was a
> hardworking freshman who was disturbed at night by
> rowdy African-American students outside his dorm
> room. He yelled at them to "shut up, you water
> buffalo"—the student was Jewish and "water buffalo"
> was likely a loose translation of the word "fool" or
> "cow" in Hebrew or Yiddish. But many interpreted
> this unusual phrase as a racist slur of some sort. A
> politically correct conflagration ensued replete with
> toxic race politics, a show trial for the offending

freshman, and enforcement of an Orwellian speech
code that prohibited any behavior "that has the
purpose or effect of . . . creat[ing] an intimidating . . .
environment," according to university regulations.

Nor did matters necessarily look up if one were faculty
rather than student. From Harvard, professor Peter Berkowitz reports:

> I recall attending a faculty gathering shortly after
> I arrived in Cambridge in which [Harvey] Mansfield
> casually—though with mischievous intent—remarked
> that it was strange that liberals could not bring
> themselves to admit that the Cold War was a *war* and
> that the United States had *won* it. As if to confirm his
> point, the jaws of Mansfield's colleagues collectively
> crashed to the ground. And, as if on cue, they cast in
> his direction a collective dirty look, a mixture of fear
> and disgust, that I had seen before: in law school when
> I would ask about the holding of the case or the text
> of the Constitution as opposed to the desirable policy
> outcome we were debating; and in graduate school
> among faculty and students when I mentioned
> [Leo] Strauss.

To what do those common threads of disbelief and revulsion and subsequent political transformation amount?

Simply this: The left/liberal monopoly on campus has had an unintended blowback indeed. It has inadvertently *created* some of the very political refugees whose work now fuels the world of conservative think tanks, journals, and ideas more broadly.

There is, finally, another factor mentioned by some contributors that is related to what drew them to the right, which is the relationship between contemporary conservatism and religious belief. Of course not all conservatives are religious, and not all religious people are conservative (as some on the left who want to harness that religiosity to Democrats are now spending a fair amount of time and money insisting). Yet as several essays in *Why I Turned Right* remind whether tacitly or otherwise, there is in fact something natural about that "fit" between the two.

There is, for one, the connection between conservatism's sense of human limitation and the similar understanding of religion. After all, the same "epistemological humility" cited by David Brooks as a pillar of his political views can be cast more widely than just the next appropriations bill. Or as P. J. O'Rourke makes the point rhetorically in discussing the largely unrecognized corollary arrogance of *dis*belief, "If I was so small that my comprehension was meaningless, what did that make my incomprehension?" Whether or not the case against God requires fewer premises than the case for atheism, it certainly requires more chutzpah—a kind of chutzpah of which many conservatives as such have learned to be suspicious.

A second reason for that fit is that religion requires something else which all nonlibertarian conservatism holds dear; it is, as Rich Lowry says, "the ultimate filial piety." And of course a third reason for that "fit"—as poet and *First Things* editor Joseph Bottum explains—was and is abortion, and how the two political parties differ in viewing that subject. For though not all conservatives (including the contributors to this book) are pro-life, many are, and they are passionately so; and what is more important, between the silencing of pro-life governor Robert Casey in 1992 and the surprise election in November 2006 of his son, who also departs from the party line on abortion, the spectacle of a pro-life Democrat was something like a celebrity sighting—an event rarely occurring in the natural order, and typically to the embarrassment of the subject.

Moreover, for some contributors and also for many other conservative Americans, abortion on demand is not only wrong in itself but also linked to other dissolutions they identify with the left. "I also began to sense a deeper flight from responsibility in the boomers," writes Richard Starr. "Their precious 'right to choose,' for instance, more and more struck me as a right not to be weighed down by any obligation to another human being. It was as if life were a big game of Monopoly and abortion was their 'get out of jail free'

card." It seems safe to say that just as some of today's conservatives appear to have been created because there was nowhere else to go intellectually, so will those who feel most powerfully about the "life" issue continue to tack right until the ideological near-monopoly on the left about abortion is broken once and for all.

≫→

To peruse these stories as editor is to hear any number of echoes of my own political journey, the same one that first led me to this book. Like most contributors, I headed off for elite education during the years when the very Western canon revered by this adolescent autodidact was being sacked by many in academic authority as purposefully (if perhaps less merrily) as Rome was by the barbarian hordes. Like contributor Heather Mac Donald, I knew enchantment and then disenchantment with the postmodernists in particular, driven sophisticates who apart from their own importance (and perhaps also the compulsive seduction of undergraduates) apparently believed in nothing, nothing, nothing—nothing at all. Like many contributors, too, I was protected by idiosyncratic factors against at least some of the ideological pathogens making the rounds. Catapulted into the Ivy League by scholarships, I felt too privileged to join ranks with the permanently aggrieved. And toward

radical feminism I proved especially immune. A sister out-
numbered by brothers, I knew unshakably that men were
more to be pitied than feared.

Most of all, however, like contributor Joseph Bottum
and scores of millions of other people, what led once and
for all and irretrievably away from the "default" zone of
liberalism in my own case was that there was no getting
around the fact of legal abortion. "Real conservatism," writes
Bottum here, "usually begins when you find in yourself
a limit, a place beyond which you will not go, and always
for me it comes back to this touchstone." And always for
me, too.

Though a lackadaisical apostate at the time, I read
Roe v. *Wade* at the suggestion of Jeremy Rabkin (then one of
Cornell's few conservative professors) and found myself
thinking, *This can't be right.* I listened over the years as one
hyphenated kind of feminist after another sounded weirdly
full-throated cheers for the routine trashing of what was obviously *some* form of human life—if not, why are we simultaneously having another national argument over using it
for spare parts?—and just as repeatedly I thought: *This can't
be right, either.* And finally it became clear, one evening while
watching a Stalinesque rigged "debate" on the subject in
which a modest local Baptist preacher was put up against a
Marcusian feminist and incessantly booed and jeered by a
mob of hundreds even though he won every point, that my
conviction had gone all the way over—to *Whatever else may*

be true or false, knowable or unknowable, this abortion thing just can't be right.

This can't be right: an intuitionist phrase does not a political philosophy make. But what started for me and, I believe, many other people weighing the real legacy of *Roe* went on to become something more—a ground-up rethinking of many other political facts that supposedly enlightened people regarded as similarly self-evident, and that turned out on inspection to be anything but. And so I moved figuratively and literally. *The Public Interest* became my surrogate graduate school and Irving Kristol, my inadvertent substitute thesis advisor—as he and other conservative and neoconservative thinkers of his generation have been for so many of the young people they hired, including some of the other writers in this book. There we imbibed what Richard Starr dubs the "parallel curriculum" that has proven to be modern conservatism's strongest asset: the essays and books of transformational thinkers such as Peter Bauer, Walter Berns, Allan Bloom, Whittaker Chambers, Robert Conquest, Midge Decter, Gertrude Himmelfarb, Sidney Hook, Paul Johnson, Jeanne Kirkpatrick, Charles Murray, Michael Novak, Norman Podhoretz, Tom Wolfe, and others. To these I would add Hannah Arendt, Christopher Lasch, Daniel Patrick Moynihan, Philip Rieff, and other iconoclasts more closely read on the right than on the left from which they hailed.

Just as reading the stories in this book as editor summons such past moments in my own parallel travels, so, too, I suspect, will many readers of *Why I Turned Right* experience similar moments of resonance. In the end, it is our collective hope that whether they are for the right or against it, enthusiastic supporters or disgusted critics, readers from all points of the spectrum will find items of interest in the pages ahead. After all, as numerous authors report, what drew them in the first place to the likes of *Commentary* and *National Review* and the *American Spectator* and *The Public Interest* and the alternative rest of the higher journalism was just that—the writing.

And so we see here, I hope. Against the dour fanaticism and calculated malice of much current commentary, this volume is intended as a modest antidote, and its pages as entertainment and perhaps even illumination for readers both red and blue.

NOVEMBER 2006
WASHINGTON, D.C.

The Unthinking Man's Guide to Conservatism

P. J. O'ROURKE

P. J. O'Rourke is a correspondent for the *Weekly Standard,*
Mencken Research Fellow at the Cato Institute, and the
author of a dozen books, including *Republican Party Reptile,*
Parliament of Whores, Eat the Rich, and a forthcoming commentary on *The Wealth of Nations* for Grove/Atlantic Press.

SOME PEOPLE ARRIVE at their political convictions through experience, some through study, some through thought. My political convictions are a result of thinking or, to be specific, lack thereof.

I was brought up in Republican circumstances, firmly grounded in convention. I was swept out to Marxist sea by a flood of sex. I was trying to impress cute beatnik girls. Then, one day, I found myself washed up on the shore of jobs and responsibilities, and I was a Republican again. No cognition, cogitation, or will seems to have been involved in my ideological spindrift. As both a radical and a reactionary I was moved by the forces of history and institutions. All those beatnik girls had a history. And many of them wound up institutionalized.

Think of me as Michael Oakeshott without a brain.

My maternal great-grandfather owned a farm in downstate Illinois. He was a county sheriff, a stalwart of the GOP, a friend of President McKinley's, and a breeder of harness racing horses. His dying words summarize my family's attitude toward the great sociopolitical issues that would shake the twentieth century: "How did Shorty do at the track today?"

His daughter, my grandmother, was ten when she began accompanying her father to Republican conventions. She never got over the shock of that blowhard easterner, Teddy Roosevelt, splitting the party and allowing such a man as Woodrow Wilson—from a Confederate state!—to become chief executive. As far as my grandmother was concerned, William Howard Taft was the last real Republican. In a moment of childish innocence I once asked her what the difference was between Republicans and Democrats. She said, "Democrats rent."

My father's family was, if anything, more Republican. My paternal grandfather was widowed and left with a business to run and six small children on his hands. He remarried more in haste than wisdom. The stepmother was insane. She left Uncle Joe out on the back steps until his diapers froze. Grandpa divorced her. Then as now there was a political aspect to getting an annulment. (The Kennedys seem to have a vending machine that dispenses them.) According to family lore, Grandpa and the local bishop clashed, and Grandpa went out and, in one day, joined the Methodist church, the Freemasons, and the Republican Party. He had a heart attack just before the 1960 election. At the funeral his sister, my great-aunt Helen, said, "It's a good thing your grandfather died when he did. It would have killed him anyway to see John Kennedy president."

Thus my life would have gone along perfectly well, politically speaking, if it hadn't been for girls. I found them interesting. They found me less so. On my first weekend at college I was walking down an alley that had a bar on either side. Each bar had a patio full of students. The girls on one patio were very attractive, their sweaters well-filled, their pleated skirts worn daringly above the knee, their blond hair styled in what was called a "sorority flip." They sipped demurely from beer mugs decorated with Greek letters.

But I wasn't athletic or handsome or a Sigma Chi legacy. And I had a feeling that, even if I were, getting such girls into bed would involve attendance at mixers and dances, romantic chat-up, fumbling under coats in the shrubbery while a house mother tsked out a window, bestowal of one's fraternity "pin" or even an engagement ring, and lots of talk about "our future."

The girls on the other patio were fetching as well, in their black leotards and peasant blouses, denim skirts and sandals. Their long, dark hair was ironed straight. They strummed guitars, smoked unfiltered cigarettes, and drank beer straight from the bottle. I thought, "I'll bet those girls do it."

They did. I went home at Christmas break with my hair grown long, wearing a blue-jean jacket with a big red fist emblazoned on the back. My grandmother said, "Pat, I'm worried about you. Are you becoming a Democrat?"

"Grandma!" I said. "Lyndon Johnson and Richard Nixon are both fascist pigs! Of course I'm not a Democrat! I'm a communist!"

"At least you're not a Democrat," said Grandma.

Having donned the clown costume, I found it easy to honk my dogma nose, squirt the progressive seltzer, and pile into tiny cars (VW bugs). Soon I really was a communist, unless I really was an anarchist or an anarcho-syndicalist or a Trotskyite or a Maoist. I never read any work of political ideology unless by accident, if it was assigned in class. And then I studied it as perfunctorily as any Sigma Chi in the lecture hall. Nothing ensures an obliviousness to theory like the need to get a passing grade on a quiz about it.

I have ex-leftist friends who recall long, intense, fractious political arguments from their university years. But I was at Miami of Ohio, not Berkeley or Columbia. My college friends and I may have begun such discussions, but then the rolling papers were brought out and the debate became over where to get Mallomars.

However, inchoate ideas are often more deeply held than any others. Emerson, for instance, was fanatical about his conception of metaphysics even though, on inspection, he didn't have one. And it's often forgotten what instinctive communal levelers and utopians kids are. After all, they're raised in the one economic organization, the family, that actually adheres to the credo of "from each according to his ability, to each according to his need." They spend their formative years under authoritarian, antimaterialist regimes at school, catechism, summer camp, and Little League. They're taught sharing and caring and fairness and a kind of toadying social equality (". . . it's how you play the game"). They're given employment consisting of involuntary volunteer work to fulfill their Boy Scout or Girl Scout or church or school community service requirement. Maybe they get a job doing some mindless sorting at Dad's friend's Kinko's. They are "part of the solution" and/or they experience proletarian alienation. Then they're sent off to college to learn about freedom and responsibility—freedom to get naked and stoned and responsibility to turn down their stereo after 1:00 A.M. It's a wonder that anybody under twenty-five is even a Mikhail Gorbachev.

And in my day there was also the war in Vietnam. Proponents of the present war in Iraq (myself included) should consider the effect that certain armed conflicts can have on the ideologically impressionable (whether at Berkeley or the University of Tehran). Wars need clear arguments of justification, clear strategies of execution, clear objectives. PS, they need to be won. And the impressionable can't be left wondering just who the winners are. World War I was a dilly in all these respects, with ideological consequences less trivial than the 1960s.

The Vietnam War's draft lent solipsism to the melo-drama of being an adolescent radical. The government was intent on interrupting my fun to send me to some distant place with a noxious climate to shoot people I didn't know, and, what was worse, they'd shoot back. I had a stepfather at home whom I was perfectly willing to shoot while he snored on the couch. But the government was insensitive to my needs.

I stayed a left-winger for more than a decade. This de-spite at least three Road to Damascus moments when I should have been converted to better views.

Moment One: During graduate school in Baltimore I worked on an "underground" newspaper. We shrilly de-nounced war, injustice, and this and that. One evening our office was invaded by a group of young people more radical than ourselves who felt that our denunciations weren't shrill enough. They called themselves, and I am not kidding, the "Balto-Cong." They accused us of being capitalist tools and said they were liberating the oppressor's private property in the name of the people. We explained that they were wel-come to it, the private property consisting of about ten thousand dollars in debt, three typewriters, and an old row house from which we were about to be evicted. (Radicals not only rent but are in arrears on it.) We were held at knuckle-point and made to undergo a consciousness raising session that might have gone on who-knows-how-long if a couple of "the people" hadn't stopped by. These were two teenage black kids from the neighborhood. They asked, "What the hell's going on here?" and scared the Balto-Cong away. The neighborhood kids were honors English students who hoped the underground newspaper would provide a venue for their poetry. And I'm glad to say that, thereafter, it did.

A fellow ex-staffer at the newspaper (now also a Republican) tells me that I spent the rest of that night slamming my fist on things and saying, "Spiro Agnew was right!" But I got over it. I had realized there were bad people on the left, but I hadn't realized I was one of them.

Moment Two: Then my student deferment ran out, and I was drafted. Standing in my underwear at the draft physical I noticed that I and all the other hirsute children of privilege were clutching thick folders of doctors' letters about asthma, neurosis, back problems, and allergies to camouflage colors. The poor kids with their normal haircuts and their discount-store Y-front briefs that came up over their navels were empty-handed and about to be marched off to war. This told me something about what my radicalism was doing to unchain the masses. But I forget what, because the army doctor told me something more interesting. He told me to get out of there. The army had no use for drug-addled hippies.

Moment Three: I remained determined that wealth should be shared with everyone, especially me. But the silent majority tacitly refused to agree, and I had to get a job. The pay was $150 a week. I was to be paid every two weeks. I eagerly looked forward to my check for three hundred dollars (as did my landlord). But when payday came I found that, after withholdings for federal, state, and city income tax, Social Security, health insurance payments, and pension plan contributions, I netted about $160. Here I'd been struggling for years to achieve socialism in America only to discover that we had it already.

Usually when I'm asked what made me a Republican I tell that story. But it isn't true. I mean the story is true, but it didn't really change my mind. I went on for years considering myself to be at least nominally a leftist.

But I was too busy to be involved in left-wing causes anymore. I had that job. And, truthfully, all causes are boring. They are a way of making yourself part of something bigger and more exciting, which guarantees that small, tedious selves are what a cause will attract. Plus I was finding my work to be about as big and exciting a thing as my own small, tedious self could handle.

And I had begun to notice something about left-wing causes. Radicals claim to seek what no one claims to want. The collective has been tried in every conceivable form from the primitively tribal to the powerfully Soviet, and "the people" who are thus collectivized immediately choose any available alternative, whether it's getting drunk on the Indian reservation or getting shot climbing the Berlin Wall.

I'd enjoyed all the left-wing rioting. Better yet had been the aftermath back at the crash pad. "We've got to get this tear gas off us. So we'd better double up in the shower, Sunshine, to conserve earth's resources." But the rioting, along with the Vietnam War, was petering out. Still, I was a man of the left. That was the sort of person I admired. Rick, in *Casablanca,* was a man of the left, and, uh, Rick in *Casablanca.* . . . Anyway, nobody gets misty-eyed singing "I dreamt I saw Bill Taft last night/As fat as he could be . . ."

I suppose a certain notion of "fairness" also continued to bother me. Now that I'm a father I try to nip that in the bud. My eight-year-old daughter is, of course, much inclined to make the statement "That's not fair!" Whenever she does, I tell her, "Honey, you're cute. That's not fair. You're smart. That's not fair. Your parents are pretty well-off. That's not fair. You were born in America. *That's* not fair. You had better pray to God that things don't start getting fair for you."

In the end it was boredom and silliness, not reason, that turned me back into a Republican. One day in the middle 1970s I was walking along a street and my reflection was caught at an odd angle in a store window so that I saw myself without realizing who I was looking at. I was wearing jeans and a work shirt with mystic chick embroidery on it and a thrift-shop military jacket and my hair was all over the place. I thought, "That guy's looking pretty silly for somebody his age."

And my friends were boring. They continued to be convinced that everything was going to be shared soon, so they hadn't gotten jobs. They hadn't gotten married either, although wives were the one thing that did seem to be getting shared. Occasionally they had a kid. They didn't let the diapers freeze. There weren't any. These children, though provided with remarkable freedom from discipline and conformity, didn't seem to give much thanks for it—or ever say thanks, or please, or even "How are you?" My friends were leading the lives of unfettered bohemian artists. Except the lack of fetters seemed to tie them to dumps on the Lower East Side (rented, not owned). And where was the art?

These people not only had a great capacity to be boring, they had a great capacity to be bored. Imagine a talent for ennui so well developed that you could be bored by God. It's a redundancy for a political radical to believe in God because politics has all of God's power to shape life and then some. God recused himself in the matter of free will. Radicals do not. Then there's the egotism of the ideal. If the problems of the world can be intellectually solved by me, what's the intellectual need for Him? Furthermore, the wicked world is so full of wrongs, which radicals need to right, making radicals better than that no-good God who created the wicked world. Or would have if He existed. God's like, you know, a square.

My own lack of religious faith persisted even after I'd renewed my faith in other things such as buying instead of renting. If I could summon enough faith to vote for the average Republican—which, by the early 1980s, I was doing—I certainly should have been able to summon enough faith for the Apostles' Creed. But the selfish leftist habit of doubt stayed with me. In 1984 I was in Lebanon writing an article about the civil war. My friend, Charlie Glass, ABC's Middle East correspondent, dragged me out into the Bekaa Valley to interview a terrifying man named Hussein Mussawi, head of a fundamentalist Shiite militia called Islamic Amal. Mussawi looked at me and asked, "Do you believe in God?" I remember wondering if I was fibbing when I very quickly said yes.

Then one day it seemed silly *not* to believe in God. Maybe existence was pointless, though it did have its points for me—writing books, fixing up the house I'd bought in New Hampshire. I'd started hunting again. I'd learned to ski. Maybe I was just too small a part of creation to understand what the larger point was. But if I was so small that my comprehension was meaningless, what did that make my incomprehension? Also, although I could imagine that existence was pointless, I couldn't imagine that it was accidental. Existence seemed too intricately organized. Having led an accidental existence for years I knew that such an existence was not very. (How often leftists need to admonish themselves with the slogan "Organize!") If the random forces of quantum physics were all that were in play then these forces had dropped butter and eggs and mushrooms and cheese and a lit match on the kitchen floor and gotten an omelet. Whether I liked omelets was neither here nor there.

On the other hand, it was just such an incredulity about things somehow organizing themselves that kept me from embracing all the implications of the free market. "Laissez faire" was a personal attitude long before I gave it larger significance. Then I remembered the lesson of my leftist days, "The personal is the political." And I began leaving other people alone not only in my life but in my mind.

By the early 1990s my political philosophy was completely elaborated. I didn't have one. I think it is the duty of every politically informed and engaged person to do everything he or she can to prevent politics.

But I was not yet a conservative. I was a Republican and a libertarian. The mutual exclusivity of those two political positions was, I thought, one more proof of the self-negating nature of politics, which should be allowed to take its course until politics is regarded as such a nugatory enterprise that people have to be chased through the streets and tackled and forced to serve as senators, representatives, presidents, and Supreme Court justices. Or maybe, I thought, there should be a game of governance tag where someone has to stay a congressman until he's able to catch someone else and make him "it." If this means legislative halls filled with the helpless and crippled, so much the better.

I still think it's a good idea. But that is not conservatism. I became a conservative at 11:59 P.M. on December 4, 1997, the way many people become conservatives. My wife gave birth. Suddenly all the ideal went out of any idealism for change. Every change reeked of danger or, in the case of diaper changes, just reeked. If the temperature in the nursery changed, I worried. If the temperature in the infant changed, I agonized. Changing my shoes became a point of anxiety. Better go to work in my slippers—any noise could wake the baby. I was tortured by the change from a child who sat up to a child who crawled. Was her speed of development too slow? Was her speed headfirst into the table leg too fast? The change from crawling to toddling was purgatory. I wanted to stand with Bill Buckley athwart the tide of history shouting, "Don't swallow the refrigerator magnet!"

Things that once were a matter of indifference became ominous threats—refrigerator magnets and gay marriage. I used to consider erotic preferences a matter of laissez faire. Then I realized, if my children think homosexuality is acceptable, it could lead them to think something really troubling—that sex is acceptable. Daddy has been down that alley. It took me years to figure out how to be a Republican again. There will be time enough for my kids to learn the facts of life from the priest during pre-Cana counseling. As for public education's "tolerance" curriculum, the heck with *Heather Has Two Mommies.* How about *Heather Has Two Nannies*—there's a book that could teach children something worthwhile in the way of values.

I have lost all my First Amendment principles about rap song lyrics. I am infuriated by them. I cannot understand a word that hip-hop musicians say. For all I know what's spewing out of their mouths is, "We need a single-payer national health care system," or, "Home mortgage interest tax deductions subsidize suburban sprawl, increasing the burden on transportation infrastructure and leading to greater production of greenhouse gases."

I am appalled by violence on TV, specifically the absence of it on PBS. "Which perfectly harmless thing is Caillou terrified of today?" I always ask my younger daughter. Why isn't he ever terrified of something sensible like a pit bull? Why don't his parents just give him a whack when he whines?

And what if a purple Tyrannosaurus rex shows up in my backyard? The kids will run outside expecting to play games and sing songs, and they'll be eaten. What kind of life lessons is PBS teaching our children?

Being a parent means suddenly agreeing with Pat Buchanan about everything except immigration. For Pete's sake, Pat, nannies are hard enough to find. Not that I want to do away with Barney, Snoop Dogg, or love (whether it can't speak its name or can't shut up). I am a true conservative. I hate *all* change.

Conservatives want things to remain exactly the way they are, not because these things are good but because these things are there. If I have to deal with them I know where they live. Conservatives are opposed to change not because change is bad but because change is new. It's modern and confusing. I don't know how to work the remote. And I can't find the off button.

Change is different. No one without children knows how fraught the word "different" is. When used about your child it's never good news. When used by your child it isn't either. If a kid says, "You're different," he means you're crazy. If he says, "I don't want to be different," he means he's going to skip school and shoplift. And when "the spaghetti tastes different," he's about to throw up.

Radicals seek to make a difference. To the born-of-parenting conservative this sounds like as much fun as seeking head lice.

And the conservative parent feels the same way about those small, itchy things called ideas. Radicalism is the pursuit of ideas (a pursuit that, for me, was made all the more tantalizing by the fact that I never came close to grasping one). Any conservative can tell you that ideas have consequences. Who wants consequences? Conservatism is a flight from ideas. As in, "Don't get any ideas," "What's the big idea?" and "Whose idea was that?"

A flight from ideas might sound like Philistinism, but think how valuable those phrases are when used on children. Or politicians. And what's so bad about being a Philistine? Putting religious prejudice aside, the Philistines seem to have been respectable people who did well in business. For all we know, the reporting on the David-Goliath battle comes down to us from some Old Testament version of NPR. And David, what with the poems, the messy love life, the increased centralization of government, was too liberal for my taste.

Furthermore, ideas are not to be confused with facts. One of the great things about being a conservative is that when a decision has to be made—for example, is hiding your spinach under your dinner plate and then trying to feed it to the dog right or wrong?—facts can be consulted. Does it violate the Ten Commandments? Is it a cardinal sin? A venial sin? Against the law? Or you can just ask Mom. A radical can't do this, no matter how many moms are extant. Radicals have to work everything through *de novo*. Radicals have ideas about sin, law, and motherhood. And the more obscure the ideas, the more difficulty in feeding them to the dog.

The great moral principles of conservatism, if not self-evident, have at least been entered into evidence by thousands of years of human experience. And the great political principles of conservatism are simple. I call them "The Clinton Principles" after those two simple souls who once occupied the White House and may yet again: "Mind your own business and keep your hands to yourself." (As Bill tells Hillary, "Mind your own business." As Hillary tells Bill, "Keep your hands to yourself.") Then there are the great intellectual principles of conservatism, which are, mmm . . .

Several years ago I was enjoying the conservative pleasures of a driven pheasant shoot in Ireland. Among my hunting companions was a wonderful old fellow named Preston Mann, now pursuing game in paradise. Preston was one of the world's great dog trainers, the proprietor of a splendid hunting club in Michigan, and a crack shotgunner. I'm none of those, particularly the last. I kept missing the pheasants with my first barrel. I generally picked them up with a second shot, but bird after bird escaped my initial blast. Preston was shooting from the next butt and, midst the flap and cackle of pheasants winging toward us, he turned to me and shouted, "P.J., you're thinking about it. It ain't a thinking man's game."

Killer Rabbits and the Continuing Crisis

RICHARD STARR

Richard Starr has been a managing editor of the *Weekly Standard* since the magazine's launch in 1995. He previously worked as an editor at a variety of publications, including the *Washington Times, The National Interest, The Public Interest, Insight,* and the *American Spectator.*

JIMMY CARTER MADE me the conservative I am today, as I suspect he did many members of my generation. In 1980, when I was nineteen, I cast my first presidential vote for Ronald Reagan. I don't think any vote since then has given me as much pleasure. Indeed, I will probably always think of myself as a Reaganite, just as millions of Americans from an earlier generation spent their lives as FDR Democrats. But I was an anti-Carter conservative before I became a Reagan Republican—for reasons that, truthfully, came as much from the gut as from the head.

I had a visceral reaction against the moral chaos and defeatism of the 1970s. It may well be that I overreacted to what I saw as a world careening off its rails. When you're young you have no accumulated scar tissue and therefore feel wrongs more acutely. You have no sense of history and therefore lack perspective. You are hypersensitive to injustice. Nonetheless, it still seems to me that if you had a patriotic bone in your body, there was no end of things to be depressed about—and deeply outraged by—in the 1970s: the U.S. surrender in Vietnam and the abandonment of our allies there; the unchecked spread of terrorism; the reign of terror by the communists in Cambodia and Vietnam; the rise of the OPEC cartel, with its massive transfer of wealth from the working people of the world to grotesquely self-indulgent Arab princelings; the Iranian revolution and hostage crisis; the Soviet invasion of Afghanistan. As a world-weary Telly Savalas said in one *Kojak* episode, "It was a bad day for the good guys." Make that a bad decade for the good guys.

Every unhappy story had an even unhappier ending. There was the Black September kidnapping of Israeli athletes at the 1972 Munich Olympics, which ended in their massacre. There were the botched rescue attempts by the U.S. military—in 1975, when the Cambodian Khmer Rouge seized the USS *Mayaguez,* and again in 1980, when the raid to free the U.S. hostages in Iran ended with the wreckage of seven U.S. helicopters in the desert and eight troops dead. There was the slow-motion catastrophe in Southeast Asia following the U.S. withdrawal; by decade's end some three million Vietnamese and Cambodians either had been murdered or had fled their homes for an uncertain fate in refugee camps and on the high seas.

I can remember just one piece of genuinely cheering news from those years, when evil received its due and justice prevailed. On July 4, 1976, a team of Israeli commandos flew two thousand miles in four transport planes to Entebbe airport in Uganda, where a group of Palestinian and German terrorists—with the connivance of Ugandan dictator Idi Amin—were holding Israeli and Jewish passengers from an Air France plane they had hijacked. The rescue was a dazzling success. The commandos killed all the hijackers and a few dozen of Amin's troops who got in the way, freeing one hundred hostages. Only two hostages were killed in the crossfire at the airport. A third, seventy-five-year-old Dora Bloch, who had been hospitalized, was dragged from her bed and murdered on orders from an enraged Idi Amin, in retaliation for the successful raid. It is emblematic of the moral swamp on the shores of the East River in Manhattan, then as now, that the U.N. Security Council deadlocked over whether to condemn the terrorists for their hijacking, or the Israelis for "violating Uganda's sovereignty."

That same day, as it happened, was the American bicentennial. Maybe it was all the Uncle Sams riding unicycles in the parades—I've always hated unicycles—but I remember being vaguely disturbed by the celebration. It felt forced, like a beloved relative had just died yet the birthday party was still going to go on, to keep up appearances for the children.

≫→

Jimmy Carter's campaign biography that summer immodestly asked, "Why Not the Best?" It soon turned out that he was an immodest man with a lot to be modest about. He had astutely positioned himself as a cultural conservative, and a man of unimpeachable ethics. He may have been that, but he was also quickly in over his head. And he proved to have no sense of natural dignity to fall back on when he was overwhelmed by the demands of the office. Bill Clinton, who famously answered MTV's "boxers or briefs" question, was not the first president to discuss his underwear in public. Jimmy Carter holds that distinction. His first act in office was to urge everyone to turn their thermostats down to sixty-five to conserve energy (fifty, if you had a fireplace). "I'm wearing heavy underwear," the president told the Associated Press on January 30, 1977. "The White House is cold inside." He confided that First Lady Rosalynn Carter had "shed a few tears" before getting used to cold in their new home.

Outside, though, it was warming up. The struggle between the hawks and doves of the Democratic Party had been going on for ten years, and was continuing inside Carter's cabinet. But in his first major foreign-policy address, at the 1977 Notre Dame commencement, he came down resoundingly on the side of the doves. Carter announced that we were standing down in the Cold War, that he was suspending the U.S. policy of containing Soviet expansion, because we were now free of the "inordinate fear of communism." He announced his "hope to persuade the Soviet Union that one country cannot impose its system of society upon another, either through direct military intervention or through the use of a client state's military force, as was the case with Cuban intervention in Angola." That was a vain hope. As history shows, one country certainly can impose its system of society upon another through direct military intervention. And on Carter's watch, Moscow would continue trying, with more or less success, in places as diverse as Afghanistan, Ethiopia, Mozambique, South Yemen, Nicaragua, and Grenada, among others. Meanwhile, respect for U.S. power around the world fell to a low ebb. Certainly, no enemy of the United States any longer had an inordinate fear of America.

Perhaps there had been a clue of what was to come in Carter's acceptance speech at the 1976 Democratic convention, when he promised to be a president who "feels your pain." We had not yet become accustomed to decoding therapy-speak, so it was possible to take this as a signal that he understood the source of our pain—we had lost our national self-respect. It was possible to think he intended to do something about alleviating that pain. That, however, was not what he intended at all. He ultimately thought that the pain was necessary, even good for us, and that his job was to help us adjust and grow accustomed to America's reduced stature in the world. Carter had run for office as an ostentatiously "born again" evangelical, and he gave the impression of believing that there was a redemptive silver lining for America in its failures. Just as personal setbacks can help individuals to cultivate the Christian virtues of humility and meekness, he seemed to believe that the setbacks America suffered under his command were turning us into a better nation.

Four years later, at the Democratic National Convention in New York City in August 1980, he put it this way in his bid for re-election: "We've learned the hard way about the world and about ourselves. But we've matured and we've grown as a nation and we've grown stronger. We've learned the uses and the limitations of power. . . . Some would argue that to master these lessons is somehow to limit our potential. That is not so. A nation which knows its true strengths, which sees its true challenges, which understands legitimate constraints, that nation—our nation— is far stronger than one which takes refuge in wishful thinking or nostalgia." Notice the emphasis on *limitations* and *constraints*—that was the pure Carter zeitgeist. Yes, he felt your pain, and he thought you should buck up and get used to it.

>>→

Being a less evolved organism, I had a more primitive reaction: Recoil from pain, seek pleasure. In the fall of 1979, when I was a freshman at Indiana University, I came across a copy of the *American Spectator,* then an up-and-coming national political monthly, though published locally. I would learn that it had been started as a student publication in Bloomington twelve years before, in reaction to the takeover of the student government by a left-wing slate of SDS members. The *Alternative,* as it was called in 1967, specialized in mockery. The first issue weighed in on the issue of war and peace with a bomb on the cover and the headline: "Drop It." It featured bad verse parodying Rod McKuen by a purported undergraduate named "Mary Qwaint" (actually written by a student named Steve Tesich, who would later earn renown as the screenwriter of *Breaking Away* and other movies). But as was explained in the fine print of the masthead, tongue only partly in cheek, "By November 1977 the word 'alternative' had acquired such an esoteric fragrance that in order to discourage unsolicited manuscripts from florists, beauticians, and other creative types" the magazine was rechristened the *American Spectator.* As the magazine was a newsprint tabloid with woodcut illustrations, it gave the appearance of being a funnier, right-wing version of the solemn and self-important left-wing *New York Review of Books.*

The *Spectator* was full of mockery, but had also branched out into serious, highbrow literary journalism.

The first issue I picked up featured on the cover a review essay of Robert Dallek's *Franklin D. Roosevelt and American Foreign Policy* by the Seton Hall diplomatic historian Edward S. Shapiro. There was a several-thousand-word excerpt from George Gilder's forthcoming *Wealth and Poverty*. (*"Wealth causes poverty*—an idea that has burst like blinding sunlight in the mind of many a young radical and still shines brightly for all who seek some alternative to hard work, thrift, inequality, and free exchange as a way of escaping want. How much easier it is—rather than learning the hard lessons of the world—merely to rage at the rich, and even steal from them.") There was a long review of the emerging literature on the "lessons of Vietnam" by Harvard's Stephen Rosen with an interesting conclusion: We should not give up protecting nations from external threats, particularly by the Soviet Union and its proxies. ("Certainly there are Persian Gulf states that would be grateful for some protection against Iraqi or Soviet attack, even if we could not protect them from internal subversion. The United States is well equipped, morally and militarily, to protect independent, sovereign nations, and poorly equipped to win hearts and minds.")

None of those worthy pieces caught my eye like the column called "The Continuing Crisis," whose author was identified merely as "RET." A flavor: "Mid-August to mid-September. Summer deliquesces into fall, and the legend of the Carter administration waxes in grandeur. Schoolchildren will someday listen agape to tales about the time our President packed the presidential toothbrush and embarked on an eight-day cruise down the Mississippi on the luxurious *Delta Queen.* As fellow passengers struggled for sleep and shouted for the captain, our President took matutinal jogs around the deck, thwacking out two miles in the decidedly dubious time of 13 minutes. While alone in a canoe, he was attacked by what every canoeist dreads, an amphibious rabbit whose deadly incisors would have slashed right through his jeans were it not for the fact that our President is a graduate of the Naval Academy and therefore trained to thwart every sort of nautical calamity."

I'm afraid I made a spectacle of myself in the library where I read this, suppressing snorts of laughter. Ridiculing a president was not exactly novel, of course. *Saturday Night Live* had dined out on the pratfalls of Jerry Ford for the duration of his short presidency. And RET's literary model, H. L. Mencken, had turned out reams of such writing a half century before. But humor is inexplicable. I can say the effect this had on me in October 1979 was transcendent. I didn't know who this RET character was, but here, at last, was someone who *did* feel my pain. And relieved it.

»→

Six months later, in the spring of 1980, I saddled up my Su-zuki Go-Fer and putt-putted from my dorm on the east side of Bloomington, Indiana, to the offices of the *American Spectator* on the courthouse square downtown. At that point, it would have been day 150-something of captivity for the fifty-two Americans being held by the Ayatollah Khomeini's student followers in Tehran, and national humiliation was becoming routine. Ted Koppel's temporary new show "America Held Hostage," which had been covering the story of the American diplomats seized in Iran every night since the previous November, had just been rechristened *Nightline* for the long haul. A gallon of gas was $1.25 at the pumps—a little over $3.00 in today's prices—not that I minded. I was interviewing for a job at my favorite magazine that—at $3.50 an hour—would more than cover the gas costs for my glorified mo-ped.

The *American Spectator* then was an exuberant mix of highbrow and lowbrow, perfectly reflecting the personality of its founder and editor-in-chief, R. Emmett Tyrrell, Jr., the RET mentioned above. Bob Tyrrell was a jock, a competitive swimmer who had been recruited to Bloomington from the suburbs of Chicago by the legendary coach Doc Counsilman, whose IU teams won six NCAA championships and whose swimmers (most famously Mark Spitz) won dozens of Olympic medals. The swimmers at IU when I was there were probably the rowdiest and the most intel-

ligent of the many athletes on campus. Bob fit the type. He
was a wiseass and a towel-snapper, but intellectually ambitious, with an Irish twinkle in his eye when he looked across
the top of his half-glasses, and an endless appetite for travel
to New York, Washington, and the capitals of Europe, where
he would seek out and assiduously pay court to his heroes,
mostly political essayists and other editors. In Europe he
would call on Luigi Barzini, Jean-François Revel, Malcolm
Muggeridge. In New York, William F. Buckley, Jr., Irving
Kristol, Norman Podhoretz, and Midge Decter. In Washington, Meg Greenfield, his editor at the *Washington Post*. He
was a snappy dresser and aspiring bon vivant, and would
seek out distinguished specimens of the type: Tom Wolfe in
New York; Taki in London. God only knows what all these
people made of Bob when he would come calling once or
twice a year from this unlikely magazine that had somehow
sprung up amid the cornfields of Indiana. There was no one
else like him.

With a succession of talented young managing editors,
Bob ran an astonishingly ecumenical magazine. He published everyone from eighteen-year-olds (movie reviewer
John Podhoretz) to eighty-year-olds (philosopher Sidney
Hook). His pages were open to all varieties of right-wing
thinker, from Old South Agrarians to New York intellectuals, from Mittel Europa nostalgists to libertarians, to apostles of the high-tech entrepreneurial future. And though the

magazine was decidedly conservative, its contributors were just as often liberal historians like Bob's academic mentor in Bloomington, the Truman biographer Robert Ferrell, Scoop Jackson Democrats, and young Social Democrats from the anticommunist wing of the labor movement. Only Mc-Governites, feminists, and the humorless hard left need not apply. If the mix seems familiar now, it's because this same collection of types would soon come together in the Reagan coalition, which was prefigured, in miniature form, in Bob's pages.

As for the lowbrow side of the operation: that's the job I was applying for, and got. My interview with publisher Ron Burr was for a part-time position to fill orders for the magazine's line of T-shirts, beer mugs, buttons ("Nixon's the One—in 1980") and bumper stickers. There were four of the last, each a parody of a then-fashionable liberal slogan: "Caution: I Speed Up for Small Animals"; "Have You Slugged Your Kid Today?"; "Nuke the Whales"; and, the most wordy and the most popular, "Nuclear Plants Are Built Better than Jane Fonda."

Unlike some other contributors to the present volume, I can't say that my intellectual trajectory has gone from left to right. But it most assuredly has headed in an upward direction.

≫→

The advantage of working for a small magazine with a high turnover in the support staff is that eventually you get a chance to do every job—from sorting the mail and dropping the boss off for his afternoon handball game, to setting type, proofing copy, writing headlines, and editing. One of my earliest editorial tasks was retyping Sidney Hook's review of Norman Podhoretz's *The Present Danger.* Being a frugal professor, Sidney had written the review longhand, filling four or five college examination blue books, without striking out more than one or two words along the way.

Though I was a student carrying a full load of classes, the magazine work provided a parallel curriculum: I read the books written by our contributors, the books they recommended, the works they alluded to in passing. In his Nobel lecture Saul Bellow perfectly described the kind of "contrary undergraduate" I was. "It was my habit," said Bellow, "to register for a course and then to do most of my reading in another field of study. So that when I should have been grinding away at 'Money and Banking' I was reading the novels of Joseph Conrad." In my case it was the novels of Evelyn Waugh and Kingsley Amis, the old magazine essays of Irving Kristol and Norman Podhoretz, the four volumes of Orwell's collected essays and journalism, the complete works of Tom Wolfe and, for light reading, *National Lampoon* and *Car and Driver.* I never took to Mencken (despite Bob's proselytizing). I was fascinated for a time with Hayek. But, after Tocqueville, I never had much patience for political theory. When I first read *Witness,* I was dazzled by what a spectacular writer Whittaker Chambers had been and felt that there must have been a conspiracy among the many admirers of Alger Hiss to cover up this basic fact.

Though I gravitated to the writings of Irving Kristol (another man who hasn't been given his due as a pure *writer*) and would later go to work for Irving at *The Public Interest,* the usual political pedigree of a neoconservative—former Trotskyite/radical/FDR liberal/Scoop Jackson acolyte— didn't remotely fit me. A year before I was typing Sidney Hook's book review I had been tending hogs on a family farm in southern Indiana. My great-uncle was elected to the State Senate in Indiana on the Prohibition Party ticket. My father knocked on doors for Goldwater in 1964. My mother joked years later that one of my father's cousins had gone on and on about a neighbor's politics one night in the 1950s, to the point where she assumed the neighbor must be a communist conspirator. Nope, just the local Democratic precinct captain. My family had the politics of the English poet Philip Larkin, who described himself to an interviewer as having always been right wing: "I suppose I identify the Right with certain virtues," he said, "and the Left with certain vices. All very unfair, no doubt. Thrift, hard work, reverence, desire to preserve—those are the virtues, in case you're wondering; and on the other hand idleness, greed and treason."

⇛→

My political beliefs have unfolded over time—some things I used to think important no longer seem to matter much, and vice versa—but my deep sympathies have always remained on the right. As I once told David Brooks, the big career choice where I grew up was between working indoors and working outdoors. I chose indoors, but I've never forgotten what it means to get your hands dirty and sweat for a living—Philip Larkin's virtues number one and two.

At the *Spectator*, I was confirmed in my revulsion at Jimmy Carter's frittering away of American power and prestige. Instead of a political conversion, I had the sensation of discovering more vivid renditions of my own inchoate feelings, and more elegant articulations of what I already believed. And I found I had joined a political community.

This allowed me to escape a university "community" that I found increasingly oppressive. It was already clear that the university was moving left. The "personal is the political" baby boomers were gaining a toehold in junior faculty positions, which they have never relinquished. The old liberal scholars were being pensioned off. The boomers had contempt for the undergraduates, who they thought should be organizing against "Ronnie Ray-gun"; we had contempt for them, preferring to spend our time at apolitical parties, and aiming our rare demonstrations at the likes of the Ayatollah Khomeini.

My clean-shaven, suit-and-tie-wearing thirtysomething bosses at the magazine, meanwhile, offered a salutary contrast to their faculty counterparts, who seemed more like aging teenagers desperate not to grow up. As I had always associated growing up with escaping the farm, I was eager for the responsibilities of adulthood, which I had correctly figured out would be less onerous than the chores of childhood. As the late John Kenneth Galbraith accurately observed, "If you have ever worked on a farm, nothing else ever seems like work."

I also began to sense a deeper flight from responsibility in the boomers. Their precious "right to choose," for instance, more and more struck me as a right not to be weighed down by any obligation to another human being. It was as if life were a big game of Monopoly and abortion was their "get out of jail free" card. "You know," I confided one day to one of my conservative friends on campus, "it was important for the baby boomers to secure abortion rights and the right to die—that way, they can kill off both their offspring and their aging parents. No one will ever have to depend on them." All very unfair of me, no doubt.

》→

Because liberals often lose elections to conservatives on the issue of national security, they have a tendency, in their solipsistic moments, to accuse conservatives of inventing national security crises to defeat them. Conservatives, they say, are always looking for an enemy—and when they can't find one they fabricate one. It's a short step from there to believing that threats are imaginary, and enemies nonexistent, which is the great modern liberal temptation.

In an essay arguing that neoconservatives had never really agreed about foreign policy, Irving Kristol a few years ago did grant that statesmen should "have the ability to distinguish friends from enemies. This is not as easy as it sounds, as the history of the Cold War revealed. The number of intelligent men who could not count the Soviet Union as an enemy, even though this was its own self-definition, was absolutely astonishing." This echoes something Daniel Patrick Moynihan said in a book describing the year he spent in the mid-1970s standing up for America at the United Nations: "I had first gone to Washington with John F. Kennedy and then stayed on with Lyndon Johnson. There I learned as an adult what I had known as a child, which is that the world is a dangerous place—and learned also that not everyone knows this."

Jimmy Carter, in his 1980 convention speech, described Ronald Reagan as inhabiting a "make-believe world, a world of good guys and bad guys, where some politicians shoot first and ask questions later. No hard choices, no sacrifice, no tough decisions—it sounds too good to be true, and it is." In his new history of the Iranian hostage crisis, *Guests of the Ayatollah,* Mark Bowden describes a colloquy between the hostages and their guards over the upcoming election. "Lieutenant Colonel Dave Roeder asked one of them, 'Do you know who Ronald Reagan is?'

"'He was a movie star,' the guard said.

"'Do you know what will happen to Iran if Reagan wins the election?' Roeder asked. The white-haired prisoner with the deep-set eyes and heavily lined face leaned forward dramatically, made a sudden expanding gesture with his hands, and said: 'Boom!' "

When Reagan defeated Carter, he had almost nothing to say about the hostages except to call the Iranians "criminals and kidnappers," and to add, "I don't think you pay ransom for people who have been kidnapped by barbarians."

The plane carrying the fifty-two American hostages to freedom left Iranian airspace shortly after Reagan was sworn in on January 21, 1981. President Reagan announced the happy news at a congressional luncheon in the Capitol. It was a good day for the good guys, and that was just right by me.

Confessions of a Greenwich Village Conservative

DAVID BROOKS

David Brooks is a columnist with the *New York Times* and a commentator on NPR and *The NewsHour* with Jim Lehrer. He is also the author of *Bobos in Paradise* and *On Paradise Drive*.

IN 1965 MY parents took me to a "Be-In." My father was teaching English literature at New York University at the time and my mother was working on her dissertation at Columbia. We took the bus up to Central Park and gathered on the lawn with thousands and thousands of early hippies. The idea was to just come and gather and Be.

There was folk music and probably plenty of drugs and at one point the flower children gathered in an Aquarius version of a conga line. Thousands of them held hands and then took off like a long denim-clad snake, streaming across the grass and over a hillside. Then, to demonstrate their liberation from money and material things, they set a garbage can on fire and began to throw their wallets onto the flames.

We formed a Dionysian circle around the burning garbage can and I was wide-eyed at the amazingness of what was going on. But then, with my sharp five-year-old's eyes, I spotted a five-dollar bill floating out of the pyre. I broke from the circle of onlookers, snatched the bill as it floated from the fire, and shoved it into my pocket.

It was my first move to the right.

The rest of the journey took a while. I'm struck as I look back on my little political peregrination by how haphazard it's been. For the past thirty years or so I've been trying on different ideological clothes—books and schools of thought and labels—as they came upon me, searching for ones that seemed comfortable. It hasn't been a rational, self-conscious, or scientific process—testing hypotheses, thinking through problems, weighing policy options, or searching for correct answers. It's been more like a meandering journey in search of the ideological clothes that fit my intuitive view of the world.

The journey took me from high school socialism to the offices of *National Review* to where I am today: the kind of conservative some *New York Times* readers can stand, or to put it more positively, a progressive, national greatness conservative in the Hamilton-Whig-Party-Lincoln-T.R.-McCain-Giuliani mold.

I grew up in a liberal household on the edge of Greenwich Village. In third grade I was paddled for writing "Julie Nixon is a Nazi" on the chalkboard, and in fourth grade a few of the Weathermen blew themselves up in a townhouse just down the street from my school. We were not as radical as that—my parents worked for Ed Koch during his more liberal incarnations as a congressional candidate, and my first political activity was handing out leaflets for an orthodox Democratic assembly candidate named Andrew Stein—but it's probably true that I didn't meet a Republican at any point during my first decade.

It was only subconsciously that the seeds of my later drift were planted, for though I grew up in the era and atmosphere of the 1960s, I was only a few miles from where my great-grandfather had settled on the Lower East Side, and though it wasn't clear at the time, that influence was far more powerful than anything tie-dyed. My great-grandfather was a kosher chicken butcher, and his wife, who must have been formidable, raised three girls and two boys, one of whom was my grandfather, Bernard Levy.

Someone once said it takes three generations to make a career, and that's certainly true in my case. My grandfather went to City College with a thousand other hungry immigrant kids and made it to Columbia Law School and became a lawyer in the Woolworth Building, writing beautiful briefs for his firm, graceful letters to the *New York Times* on ubiquitous subjects, and eloquent notes to me when I was away at summer camp. He not only made writing seem like a field of glory, he also repeated the immigrant lectures that his mother must have delivered to him in progressively nicer apartments on the Lower East Side and then on upper Fifth Avenue during the first decades of the twentieth century.

These were lectures all immigrant kids receive, or should receive—on the importance of ambition, of making it, of climbing up the great ladder of bourgeois success and fulfilling the American dream. On the streets around Washington Square in 1969, people were rebelling against the oppressiveness of bourgeois success and conventional ambition, but on our walks along those same streets, my grandfather was instilling an opposite code.

Many of the people who turned into neoconservatives—Irving Kristol, Gertrude Himmelfarb, Norman Podhoretz—abandoned the left when it renounced the bourgeois virtues in which they had been raised. I absorbed the bourgeois culture and the antibourgeois counterculture simultaneously. I wasn't unaffected by the former—socially I drift left—but the striving immigrant creed seeped deeper into my brain, and would emerge to consciousness decades later.

≫→

When I was twelve we moved out to the suburbs of Philadelphia, and I reacted the way any New Yorker would who thought he was eminently more urbane than the suburbanites who were suddenly around him. I became a snob. That meant looking down on anyone who didn't seem as cultured, hip or liberal as I thought New Yorkers were. In my high school graduation photo I'm pictured wearing an army fatigue jacket with political buttons all over it. My heroes in those days were the right ones to have—Hubert Humphrey, Scoop Jackson, Birch Bayh—but my liberalism was really status liberalism. I took it as a matter of course that we on the left were the smart ones, not the conformists; we were the compassionate ones, not the cold, unimaginative corporate types; we were the ones who had been vindicated by history again and again and again: the New Deal, the civil rights movement, Vietnam.

Herbert Butterfield once wrote, "Over and again we discover to what degree . . . men do their thinking and form their attitudes by reference to some presumed picture of a procession of the centuries. The framework which people give to their general history—the notion they have of man in time and of their process of time—may do much to determine the rest of their outlook." In those days I assumed that the story of history was the story of liberal enlightenment gradually triumphing over conservative reaction, and that it had been that way for hundreds of years.

My first shock, and I do mean shock, came in college, at the University of Chicago, when I was assigned Edmund Burke's *Reflections on the Revolution in France.* I loathed that book. I still remember vibrating in disbelief as Burke defended obedience, tradition and prejudice. The professor who taught Burke later told me that my drift to the right proved that he'd failed as a teacher, but he was a better professor than indoctrinator. We went over each of Burke's

chapters in details and in the midst of my fury I did find a
passage that struck me as oddly compelling. It comes in the
midst of Burke's defense of what he calls just prejudices.
"We are generally men of untaught feelings, that, instead of
casting away all our old prejudices, we cherish them to a
very considerable degree," Burke writes.

Then, he adds:

> We cherish them because they are prejudices; and
> the longer they have lasted and the more generally
> they have prevailed, the more we cherish them. We are
> afraid to put men to live and trade each on his own
> private stock of reason, because we suspect that this
> stock in each man is small, and that the individuals
> would do better to avail themselves of the general
> bank and capital of nations and of ages.

I was just then being introduced to academic social science, with its vast abstract models to explain human behavior. I was thinking of majoring in philosophy, with its
abstract theories and logical game playing. All this eventually struck me as absurdly removed from the intricate and
unknowable patterns of how human beings actually are.
And here was Burke, alone among the people I was reading
at the time, telling me something fundamental that seemed
true, that our private stock of reason is small, that our capacity for understanding life through abstract reasoning is

extremely limited, that attempts to engineer society through technocratic plans and rational models of human behavior are bound to lead to disaster.

I soon found other writers arguing along similar lines: Thomas Hobbes, Isaiah Berlin, William Barrett, and eventually Michael Oakeshott. The combined message was that since we lack the means to understand the world and ourselves, wisdom consists in developing a heightened sensitivity to the landscape of reality, the way things fit together and can never fit together, the patterns that have endured and the habits that stretch back through time even if we cannot immediately understand or defend them with words.

Years later I would learn that epistemological modesty, the awareness of the limits of what we can know and express, is one of the pillars of conservatism. It is the second of the two major pillars of mine.

You may notice that these two pillars—the immigrant's striving for the American Dream, and Burkean epistemological modesty—fit together uncomfortably. One is future-oriented and the other is past-oriented. One commands you to venture out boldly into the unknown, fired by grand visions and armed with daring plans. The other counsels you to remain rooted in place, to steer away from utopian visions and constant change and ferment.

This is merely to say I am an American conservative, not a European one. Unlike our counterparts across the Atlantic, American conservatives are progressive. We believe in the lure of the future even while feeling the wisdom of the past, and sensing that we have lost virtues that our forefathers possessed. We value Reaganesque optimism even while we are pessimistic about human nature and the capacities of the human mind. We American conservatives are unlike any other conservatives. Because we are American our identities are defined by the abstract ideals of the founders, that human beings are endowed by their creators with certain inalienable rights. Because we are conservative, we are suspicious of abstractions, and social engineering. Because we are American, we believe in self-transformation, that each of us has a core obligation to rise and improve our station. Because we are conservative, we know that we are socially embedded creatures who cannot even understand how our beliefs and habits have been formed by the centuries and bestowed upon us in a thousand invisible and unspoken ways.

This tension defines American conservatism and has driven my political journey. When I've made mistakes it has been because I've drifted too far toward one of the opposing poles—restlessly embracing grand, idealistic, transformative plans when I should have been more aware of the limits on what we can know and engineer, or, on the other hand, cautiously doubting conscious willed change, when in fact sometimes it really is possible for people to make big changes for the better.

≫→

This conflict came to a head decades later in the run-up to the second war in Iraq. I continue to believe that America should seek to transform the Middle East, to aggressively champion democracy so all human beings can realize their inalienable rights. When societies are dysfunctional, and produce ideologies that terrorize the globe, there is no sense being conservative about them. Yet at the same time, I should have paid more attention to the Burkean whisperings in the back of my head, warnings that societies are organic and too complicated to be easily transformed. I should have been louder in insisting, as many so-called neocons did insist, that the United States enter Iraq with sufficient troops to fulfill the primary functions of government. I should have paid more heed to the conservative insight that human beings can turn savage when social order breaks down.

Nonetheless, I still think the foray into Iraq is one of the noblest endeavors the United States, or any great power, has ever undertaken. When American conservatism is at its best it understands the pull of these two opposing impulses—it is ambitious to chart a progressive future tempered by an awareness of what we cannot know. And it understands that there is no real way to finally reconcile the competing cries of hope and experience. We just have to keep the opposing truths alive in our minds and maneuver day by day. I still believe in the Iraq effort, but I should have listened to Burke's cautions a bit more, and understood that certain people in the U.S. government were total innocents when it comes to the complexity of foreign cultures and worlds.

By the time I graduated from college I was conservative in some form. It's just that I didn't know it. I was still living amidst liberals and assuming that every intelligent person must be one. (The University of Chicago's reputation for conservatism is vastly overblown—because I studied neither economics nor Straussian philosophy, I never met a conservative professor, and I knew only one conservative student.)

But around campus I was developing a reputation for being the conservative myself. I was writing columns for the school paper about Jesse Jackson's identity politics, and generating outraged letters to the editor from people whom I thought I agreed with. In the beginning of my junior year I recall getting into an argument with my then girlfriend during which she blurted out that I was turning conservative. I was deeply insulted.

And yet time and events eventually introduce us to who we are. I was also writing a humor column for the student paper, and one day during my senior year, William F. Buckley came to campus. Buckley had just published an excerpt from his book *Overdrive* in the *New Yorker*. The book, you may recall, described what Buckley's life was really like—one accomplishment after another, meals and meetings with famous people, luxurious vacations and glamorous limo rides—and I wrote a parody of it.

"William Freemarket Buckley was born on December 25, 1925 in a little town called Bethlehem. He was baptized on December 28th and admitted to Yale University on the 30th," I wrote. "Buckley spent most of his infancy working on his memoirs. By the time he had learned how to talk, he had finished three volumes: 'The World Before Buckley,' which traced the history of the world prior to his conception; 'The Seeds of Utopia,' which outlined his effect on world events during the nine months of his gestation; and 'The Glorious Dawn,' which described the profound ramifications of his birth on the social order."

The column went on this way for another eight hundred words or so. I noted that his ability to turn water into wine added to his popularity at prep school, that at Yale he majored in everything and wrote three books—*God and Me at Yale, God and Me at Home,* and *God and Me at the Movies.* After Yale, I noted, Buckley formed two magazines, *The National Buckley* and *The Buckley Review,* which eventually merged to form *The Buckley Buckley.*

A Chicago professor, Nathan Tarcov, gave Buckley a copy of the column, and as Buckley was delivering a lecture on campus, he interrupted himself and said, "David Brooks, if you're in the audience, I'd like to give you a job."

As it transpired, I wasn't in the audience. I had been selected to debate Milton Friedman for a TV show he was doing as a sequel to *Free to Choose.* The new series was supposed to show Friedman talking to the young, and I was one of the show's two socialists. I'd spent the previous weeks boning up on liberal economics and as the cameras rolled I regurgitated some point I had read in books by, say, Robert Lekachman. It generally took Friedman about eight words to rebut whatever I had just said, and then the camera would linger on my face as I sat there, open-mouthed, trying to think of something to say.

At night the Friedmans took us out to dinner, and Milton pushed aside his entrée (sweetbreads) and kept teaching us through the meal about his beliefs. I never became quite as libertarian as Friedman is, but the event was important because it showed me that there really were very smart people on the right, who had at least as much compassion for the poor as my liberal friends and who also championed plausible policies to help them and everyone else. Friedman's worldview also overlapped with Burke's cautions about what we can know. Though they draw different conclusions, both libertarians and conservatives are aware of what Hayek called the Fatal Conceit, that we can know enough to undertake large-scale social planning.

≫→

I returned to Chicago, worked as a bartender at the faculty club, wrote columns for an idealistic weekly that was meant to serve the black South Side of Chicago the way the *Chicago Reader* served the white North Side. I learned I didn't want to become a novelist (I helped edit a literary review called the *Chicago Review* and found the fiction world precious and claustrophobic). And I learned more about Chicago.

I spent a lot of time at political rallies on the South and West sides and got to see firsthand the effects of Great Society welfare programs. They crashed into both pillars of what would later become my conservatism. In the first place the welfare programs, as they then existed, enabled people to avoid work, to forgo the hard striving that was at the center of the immigrant ethic. Second, they, and the housing projects that preceded them, were the product of abstract, technocratic efforts to reform society that were designed by people who had no concept of the intricacies of human nature.

It's fine to throw money at the oppressed, but as many conservatives were already arguing and as I could see at the time, if you wind up undermining families, creating a culture of dependency, then you are doing more harm than good. Furthermore, these welfare policies were initiated at a time when prominent voices in the culture were rejecting bourgeois values like self-restraint, family, fidelity, and faith. The results were bound to be disastrous, and were.

So I ended up drifting right. One day in 1983, watching

the news, I realized with a shock that I admired Margaret Thatcher, a person I had always thought I despised. Then, I worked at an outfit called the City News Bureau as a police reporter, covering rapes, murder, and the like and seeing the dark underbelly of what American cities had become in the 1970s and 1980s.

In 1984, I called up Bill Buckley and asked him if that job offer was still open. He said it was and eventually I moved to New York to work at *National Review.*

What followed over the next decade was a journey from one conservative institution to another, as I tried to figure out exactly what kind of conservative I was. At *National Review* I got to watch Buckley and experience his extraordinary capacity for friendship, which is his greatest trait. I also learned about conservatism as a movement, the exodus story from the wilderness, when the movement was guided by people like Whittaker Chambers, Peter Vierek, and James Burnham, slowly, slowly to the promised land—the White House under Reagan.

I admired the people at *National Review,* but didn't quite have their faith in Natural Law. I didn't quite have their firm conviction that there is a transcendent, eternal moral order to the universe and that society should strive to be as consistent with it as possible.

Then I had a fellowship at the Hoover Institution at Stanford. At three-thirty all the scholars would come down for coffee and cookies at a common area and I could decide

each day whether I wanted to sit and listen to the econo-
mists like Friedman at one table, or the philosophers and social scientists, led by Sidney Hook, at another. I recall sitting
spellbound one day for three hours as Hook unraveled the
problem of evil.

Then, thanks to Buckley connections, it was off to
Washington to work as an editorial writer and movie critic
at the *Washington Times.* Reagan had just been re-elected and
in D.C. I met many of the people who would become lifelong friends—Robert Kagan, John Podhoretz, Nicholas Eberstadt, Andrew Ferguson, and many others. In those days the
conservative movement was still cohesive and friendly, and
I remember a series of parties with libertarians, pro-lifers,
Scoop Jackson hawks, movement activists, and movement
dissenters all dancing together to the Talking Heads, without realizing that that is what many of us would become.

I did a lot of writing in those days but really I was just
mimicking ideas I'd absorbed from my elders. I wrote many
supply-side editorials for the *Times,* admiring the energy and
optimism of the supply-siders and suppressing the doubts I
had that individuals are really that affected by changes in
marginal tax rates. Every real-life human being I've met is
influenced more by culture and the thirst for recognition
than by tax incentives and the hunger for wealth.

I came next to the attention of Robert Bartley, who
gave me a job on the editorial page of the *Wall Street Journal.*
Bartley was best described as the greatest high-wire act in

American journalism. He took incredible risks on ideas and writers, and I loved my time at the *Journal,* but at the same time I knew I was not quite the *Journal* type. Not socially conservative enough to be a *National Review* conservative, I wasn't free market enough to be a *Journal* conservative. I didn't really know what I was, but I didn't feel that government inherently impinged upon freedom. I disliked government programs that undermined good values, but I had no concerns about government programs that didn't, and I suspected that it was possible to design government programs that would actually improve conditions and character. It's sometimes said you can define a conservative by what year he or she wants to go back to. I never wanted to repeal the New Deal. It was the Great Society that was causing me problems.

What I also never understood about Bartley is what he thought about culture. He somehow knew that culture mattered, but he seemed uncomfortable writing about it. He wrote as if economic incentives shape history above all. One day, just after the fall of the Berlin Wall, I recall sitting in an editorial board meeting in which Bob observed that if the former communist nations merely secure property rights then the other good things they need will follow. I remember thinking that wasn't quite right, but as an editorial writer, it is actually hard to develop or understand your own opinions. You are there to articulate the opinions of the page, which I didn't disagree with, but which didn't feel comfortable somehow.

Bob did send me off to Europe, though, where I lived for four and a half years, from 1991 to 1995. They were glorious years for the world—the collapse of communism, the release of Mandela, the false dawn of peace in the Middle East—and for me, three thousand miles away before the age of the internet, they were a chance to do a lot of reading. I discovered two important things in Europe. First, I discovered America. Traveling around Europe and the Middle East I realized deep in my bones that America really is exceptional, and how much my own mind is a product of the mystic chords that run through American history. I became much more self-conscious about what it means to live in a new nation, a pioneer nation, an immigrant nation.

If that reinforced my grandfather's lectures, I also discovered other things in Europe that reinforced my Inner Burkean. Remember this was a time when technocratic dreams of reshaping society were collapsing in Russia and new technocratic dreams were being launched in Brussels. In this world, Michael Oakeshott's essay "On Rationalism" hit me with tremendous power.

"The politicians of Europe," Oakeshott wrote, "pore over the simmering banquet they are preparing for the future; but like jumped-up kitchen-porters deputizing for an absent cook, their knowledge does not extend beyond the written word which they read mechanically—it generates ideas in their heads but no tastes in their mouths."

That was it exactly. Oakeshott explained that while technical knowledge may be read out of books, the most important knowledge is absorbed through experience and exists only in practice. Rationalists who try to impose technocratic plans on reality never understand the problems they cause, and so it was with the European elites, trying to impose a unified technocratic state on diverse nations, trying to create a superpower with directives, but only clogging the arteries of societies and leading to stagnant growth and gradual continental decline.

I returned from Europe in 1994, followed the Gingrich revolution from New York, and then moved to Washington to help found the *Weekly Standard* with many of my friends. It was there that I really had the chance to think for myself, and to figure out what I believed. The Republican Revolutionaries had shut down the government in a fit of libertarian delusion. I began reintroducing myself to the breadth of American society, and gradually I realized that all the things that had occurred in my life—the New York cosmopolitan upbringing, the immigrant roots, disillusionment with liberal welfare policies, the rediscovered Americanism, the Burkean disenchantment with rational planning—pointed me in the direction of a tradition in American politics that once was strong but now is nearly dormant, the tradition that begins with the immigrant boy, Alexander Hamilton.

After a few decades in the fitting room, I came to see that I'm a Hamiltonian conservative.

The great debate of the twentieth century was over the size of government, between socialists and liberals who wanted big government and the libertarian-inspired conservatives who wanted small government. The Hamiltonians, who want limited but energetic government to enhance mobility and competition, sat crosswise to this debate. The tradition has nearly died.

But there are a few of us who cling to it, both in the Democratic Party—at the Democratic Leadership Council and at the Brookings Institution, where Robert Rubin and others have launched the Hamilton Project—and in the Republican Party, with John McCain, Rudy Giuliani, and many of the thinkers associated with the Manhattan Institute and elsewhere.

I'm convinced this tradition is poised for a rebound. I'm convinced that the main task ahead is to flesh out a governing philosophy that uses government in energetic but limited ways to encourage enterprise, build human capital, and establish the sort of social order that is the prerequisite for healthy individual freedom.

Sometimes people tell me they find my writing unpredictable. That's just because I sit crossways to the two party orthodoxies. Most of my writing is utterly consistent with the Hamiltonian tradition that is my resting spot after a few decades of meandering self-definition.

Recollections of a Campus Renegade

DINESH D'SOUZA

Dinesh D'Souza is the Robert and Karen Rishwain Fellow at the Hoover Institution at Stanford University. A founding editor of the *Dartmouth Review* and a former policy analyst in the Reagan administration, he is author among other books of several *New York Times* bestsellers, including *Illiberal Education* (Free Press, 1991), *The End of Racism* (Free Press, 1995), and *What's So Great About America* (Regnery, 2002). His most recent book is *Letters to a Young Conservative* (Basic Books, 2003). He is also author of *The Enemy at Home: The Cultural Left and Its Responsibility for 9/11* (Doubleday, spring 2007).

I ARRIVED AT Dartmouth in the fall of 1979, having come to the United States the previous year as a Rotary exchange student from India. Dartmouth was entirely new to me. I had never even visited the campus before; I am not even sure I had heard of it when I applied. But my host family in Arizona convinced me that it was an Ivy League institution, and that I should attend. They left out the part about the snow.

I started out at Dartmouth as a pretty typical Asian-American student. Having grown up in Mumbai in a middle-class family at a time when good jobs were very limited, I looked to the United States for its wide horizons of opportunity. My plans were to take advantage of the Ivy League education by majoring in economics and then going on to get an advanced degree in business, either in the United

States or in London. (Actually, these were my parents' plans for me, but I had made them my own.)

I enjoyed writing, however, and signed up to write for the campus newspaper the *Dartmouth.* I learned the basics of journalism and wrote several news stories during my freshman year. Toward the end of the year, a major schism occurred at "The D." The editor of the paper came out of the closet as a conservative. He began to write editorials supporting the candidacy of Ronald Reagan for president, while the other editors, scandalized by this offense, began the process of getting him fired. They succeeded, and the brash young editor, Gregory Fossedal, resolved to start an alternative weekly newspaper. He called it the *Dartmouth Review,* and modeled it after William F. Buckley's *National Review.*

I was not a conservative. I was raised in a household where politics was never discussed. My father was an engineer, and my mother a housewife. Both implanted in me a respect for knowledge and for education, but their idea of education was professional competence; it had nothing to do with liberal education. Not surprisingly, I had never heard of *National Review.* In my freshman year at Dartmouth, I saw myself as apolitical. In retrospect, I realize that by the end of the first term in college my views were mostly liberal. If you had said "capitalism" I would have said "greed." If you had said "Reagan" I would have said "washed-up former actor." If you had said "El Salvador" I would have said "Another Vietnam." If you had said "morality" I would have said

"Can't legislate it." These were not reasoned convictions. Rather, I was carried by the tide. There is a liberal current that flows on most college campuses, and the more prestigious the campus, the stronger the current. If you do not recognize this, you will surely be swept along. The only way to avoid this is to actively resist the waves.

While I had acquiesced in the prevailing liberal *Weltanschauung,* I was by no means a radical. Indeed during my freshman year I was offended by much of the radicalism on campus, although I had no coherent way to think about it or to express my dissatisfaction. For instance, during our convocation ceremony, a very dignified affair, our college chaplain said to our freshman class, "I want each of you to look to the student on your right, and the student on the left. One of the three of you will have a homosexual experience to climax before you graduate." Personally I found this a bit shocking. Indeed I looked to my left and right, and resolved to avoid those two guys for the rest of my days at Dartmouth.

I was also troubled by the radicalism of the feminist professors on campus. These women made statements to the effect that all males were potential rapists. One professor said she could barely walk around the Dartmouth campus because the tall tower of Baker Library upset her so deeply. To her, the tall buildings at Dartmouth were "phallic symbols." Apparently this woman's definition of a phallic symbol was anything that was longer than it was wide. And these women were famous for bringing their politics into the classroom, so that if you didn't agree with them your grade was likely to suffer.

Another phenomenon I found puzzling was the anti-Americanism of many foreign students. We had foreign students who were on full scholarship at one of the most beautiful campuses in the world, yet they spent their time bitterly complaining, and some even found Dartmouth responsible for their "institutional oppression." Iranian students who had been sent to America to study by the shah had now become avid supporters of the Ayatollah Khomeini, whose social policies they deplored but whose anti-Americanism they found delightful and exhilarating. At the time I did not know what to make of these things.

I joined the *Dartmouth Review* for two reasons: one esthetic, and the other intellectual. The first was that I found a style and a joie de vivre that I had not previously associated with conservatism. The best example of this was the paper's mentor, Jeffrey Hart, a professor of English at Dartmouth and a senior editor of *National Review.* Hart was the exact opposite of the conservative stereotype. He wore a long raccoon coat around campus and smoked long pipes with curvaceous handles. He sometimes wore buttons that said things like "Soak the Poor." In his office he had a wooden, pincerlike device that he explained was for the purpose of "pinching women that you don't want to touch." Rumor had it that he went to faculty meetings with his wooden-hand contraption. When a dean or professor would go on and on, Hart would churn the rotary device and the fingers on the wooden hand would drum impatiently in a clacking motion, as if to say, "Get on with it."

Even more outrageous than Hart's attire and equipment was his mind. He was a walking producer of aphorisms, and in his writing he had a way of getting right to the point. "When I heard about the French Revolution," Hart said, "my reaction was that I was against it." During a trip to Washington, D.C., a group of us passed by an antiracism demonstration. One fiery-eyed black man wearing a Malcolm X shirt approached Hart. "Hey, man," he said. "Can I have two dollars for breakfast?" Hart replied, "Shame on you. You should be using the money to fight racism."

Hart's most controversial column about Dartmouth was called "The Ugly Protesters." He wrote it during the time of the South Africa protests, when the campus green was regularly occupied by a horde of angry young men and women shouting, "End Apartheid," "Avenge the Death of Steven Biko," "No More Sharpeville Massacres," and "Divestment Now." Hart said he was puzzled by the intensity of the protesters. What possible interest could they have in events so remote from their everyday lives? Observing the protesters, Hart noted that their unifying characteristic was that they were disheveled. Not to mince words, they were, as a group, rather ugly. Exploring the connection between their demeanor and their political activism, Hart arrived at the following conclusion: They were protesting their own ugliness! Hart's column caused a sensation on campus. Walking to class the next day, I saw a remarkable sight on the Dartmouth green. In an attempt to disprove Hart's characterization, the protesters had showed up in suits and long dresses. But they had made a strategic blunder, because their suits were so ill-fitting that they looked even more ridiculous. Watching the scene from his office in Sanborn Hall, Hart blew billows of smoke from his pipe and giggled with obscene pleasure.

I remember some of those early dinners at the Hart farmhouse, where we drank South American wine and listened to recordings of Hemingway and Fitzgerald, Robert Frost reading his poems, Nixon speeches, comedian Rich Little doing his Nixon imitation, George C. Scott delivering the opening speech in *Patton,* some of Churchill's orations, and the music from the BBC version of Evelyn Waugh's *Brideshead Revisited.* There was an ethos here, and a sensibility, and it conveyed to me something about conservatism that I had never suspected. Here was a conservatism that was alive; that was engaged with art, music, and literature; that was at the same time ironic, lighthearted, and fun.

The second reason I joined the *Dartmouth Review* was that I was greatly impressed by the seriousness of the conservative students. They were passionate about ideas, and they argued vigorously about what it meant to be a conservative, and what it meant to be an American, and who was a liberally educated person, and who should belong to a liberal arts community, and whether journalism could be objective, and whether reason could refute revelation, and whether corporations should give money to charity, and why Stalin was a worse guy than Hitler, and why socialism was not merely inefficient but also immoral. One time in the middle of a serious argument I proposed a break for dinner and was greeted with the response, "We have not resolved the morality of U.S. foreign policy and you want to EAT?"

I realized that these students, who were not much older than I was, had answers before I had figured out what the questions were. My aspirations up to this point were to do well in college and to go on to get a good job, but I had never before considered the question of why the world looked the way that it did, and how it might be changed for the better. The conversations of the young right-wingers, peppered with references to classical and modern sources, revealed to me how much I could learn from them, and how much I had to learn on my own. Thus I began to read voraciously, not just my classroom fare but also Burke, Hume, Adam Smith, Fitzgerald, Waugh, Hayek, and Solzhenitsyn.

Here I discovered a range of ideas that I found very congenial. Having grown up in a culture with a strong sense of respect for the past, I liked the conservative emphasis on tradition as an accumulation of experiential wisdom and warmed to Burke's idea that organic change is in general preferable to revolutionary change. I have always had a skeptical or realistic view of human nature, and so quickly understood why force is an indispensable element in foreign policy, and why capitalism is necessary to channel human self-interest toward the material benefit of society as a whole. As a newcomer to America who was trying to make it through talent and hard work, I liked the idea of meritocracy and never viewed merit as a disguised form of racism. (Having taken standardized tests to get into Dartmouth, it didn't look to me like they were devised by the Ku Klux Klan.) Finally, without being conscious of it, I embodied the social conservatism that is characteristic of the whole swath of cultures stretching from the Middle East to China. Through my reading and discussion, gradually I found myself developing a grounded point of view. For the first time disparate facts began to fit together, to make sense. Soon I realized that on the level of core beliefs I had less in common with the guy with the Che Guevara T-shirt and more in common with the guy with the Adam Smith tie. Conservatism provided me with a framework, durable and yet flexible, for understanding the world. And having understood the world, at the tender age of twenty, I was ready to change it.

When I think about our escapades on the *Dartmouth Review,* I cannot resist a smile. As I recount some sophomoric things that we did, keep in mind that during this time we were sophomores! Now in my midforties, I have a somewhat different perspective than I did when I was twenty. Not that my views have moderated. As the parent of an eleven-year-old daughter, I am more socially conservative today than I ever have been. In fact, of late I've been thinking that I might need a gun. Even so, as a writer I am a different person than in my youth, and thus in reflecting on those happy and adventurous Dartmouth years, it seems worthwhile to ask what we accomplished. What did we gain and what did we lose, and was it worth it?

The first thing I should note is that we were an outrageous bunch. I didn't start out this way; in fact, for the first year I was considered a moderating influence on the *Dartmouth Review*. The reason I became radicalized is that I saw how harshly the conservative newspaper was treated by professors and by the administration. No sooner did the first issue appear on campus than the administration threatened to sue the *Dartmouth Review* for using the name "Dartmouth." The college maintained that it owned full and exclusive copyright to the name. Never mind that Dartmouth is a town in England. In fact, some two dozen establishments in Hanover—from Dartmouth Bookstore to Dartmouth Cleaners to Dartmouth Printing—all used the name. These were commercial operations unaffiliated with the college. By contrast, we were a group of Dartmouth students publishing a weekly about Dartmouth College and distributing it to the Dartmouth community. Clearly the motivation behind the lawsuit was ideological.

The administration did not stop with legal threats. Early in the paper's history, while one of the editors, Ben Hart, was distributing copies in the Blunt Alumni Center, a college official named Sam Smith went berserk, attacked Ben, and bit him! The way this happened was that Smith grabbed Ben from behind, Ben attempted to free himself by wrapping his arm around Smith's neck, and Smith proceeded to bite him in the chest. When Ben—who is the son of Jeffrey Hart—entered his dad's office and explained the bloody gash, his father's terse response was, "Thank God you didn't have him in a scissors hold." Smith eventually received probation and paid a small court-imposed fine.

These actions, inconsequential and even amusing in themselves, nevertheless reveal the psychology of the typical liberal college administrator. These guys are harsh, even brutal, in dealing with conservative dissent; invertebrate, even encouraging, in dealing with liberal dissent—and yet they solemnly insist that they are being fair. During my freshman year the Dartmouth administration sought to expel a reporter for the *Dartmouth Review* for "vexatious oral exchange" with a professor. Meanwhile, the left-wing radicals who took over the Dartmouth library faced no charges, and Dartmouth's president even apologized that he was out of town at the time and couldn't attend to their urgent demands. As this hollow man explained himself to the radicals, "My absence was not an attempt to be insensitive to your burning need."

These incidents point to a larger dilemma faced by conservative students in a liberal culture. The dilemma can be stated in this way: Typically, the conservative attempts to conserve—to hold on to the values of the existing society. But what if the existing society is liberal? What if the existing society is inherently hostile to conservative beliefs? It is foolish for a conservative to attempt to conserve that culture. Rather, he must seek to undermine it, to thwart it, to challenge it at the root level. This means that the conservative must stop being conservative. More precisely, he must be philosophically conservative but temperamentally radical. This is what we at the *Dartmouth Review* quickly understood.

I discovered another reason why the conservative activist on the liberal campus needs a radical approach. On elite liberal campuses like Dartmouth, politics is frequently transmitted to students not through argument but through etiquette. You see, the high school graduate who comes to an Ivy League college wants nothing more than to learn what it means to be an educated Dartmouth man (or woman). And the professors realize this, and exploit it. Consider the freshman who goes to a faculty cocktail party and says that he is concerned about "the communist plot in Nicaragua." What do the professors do? Do they argue with him? Do they seek to demonstrate that the Sandinistas are not Marxist? No, they raise their noses into the air and give the student a look as if to say, "Are you from Iowa?" The student is humiliated. He realizes that he has committed a social gaffe. And over time, he learns. By the time he is a senior he is winning big social accolades from his professors by going on about "the rising tide of homophobia that is engulfing our society."

At the *Dartmouth Review,* we recognized that in order to fully confront liberalism we could not be content with rebutting liberal arguments. We also had to subvert liberal culture, and this meant disrupting the etiquette of liberalism. In other words, we had to become social guerillas. This we set out to do with a vengeance.

Reading over old issues of the *Review,* and sharing recollections with my former colleagues, I am sometimes amazed at what social and intellectual renegades we were. We were not above using ad hominem attacks. We described one professor as sporting "a polyester tie and a rat's-hair mustache." When he wrote to complain, noting that he never wore polyester ties and that his mustache could not be reasonably compared to rat's hair, we printed an apology. "We Goofed, see p. 6." In our apology we said, "We regret our error. In reality Professor Spitzer has a rat's-hair tie and a polyester mustache."

Feminists and homosexuals were regular targets of *Review* satire. One of our columnists, Keeney Jones, observed a decade after Dartmouth went coed, "The question is not whether women should be educated at Dartmouth. The question is whether women should be educated at all."

The *Review* also printed an alumnus's Solomonic observation that "any man who thinks a woman is his intellectual equal is probably right." And the Last Word—a series of quips and quotations on the last page of the newspaper—featured the observation: *"Homosexuality is fine," said Bill, half in Ernest.*

Sometimes items from the bad-taste file at *National Review* made their way into the *Dartmouth Review*. From Jeff Hart we learned that the editors of *National Review* kept a file of jokes that they felt were too inflammatory for a respectable national magazine to print. But we found them entirely appropriate for a college weekly. Thus the *Dartmouth Review*'s obituary for actress Natalie Wood ended thus, "We deplore the foul rumor. Ted Kennedy was not on Catalina Island when Natalie Wood drowned." When the new Miss America, Vanessa Williams, was forced to give up her title following news reports that she posed nude for *Penthouse,* the *Dartmouth Review* noted, "Jesse Jackson may pull out of the presidential race this season. It has been revealed that his grandmother has been posing nude in *National Geographic.*"

That some of these quips are in bad taste goes without saying. But is this scorched-earth approach effective? Let's consider a couple of cases. When Dartmouth refused to stop funding the Gay Students Association, despite numerous *Review* editorials questioning why funds should be awarded based on sexual orientation, we decided to test the consistency of the administration's policy. We founded the Dartmouth Bestiality Society. We had a president, a vice president, a treasurer, and a zookeeper. We wrote up an application and developed a budget. Then we went before the college committee on funding and made our case.

The administrators were appalled, of course. "There is no interest in, ahem, bestiality at Dartmouth," one said. To which the president of the Bestiality Society gamely replied, "That may be true, Dean Hanson, but it is because of centuries of discrimination! Those of us who are inclined toward animals have been systematically excluded and ostracized. Our organization will provide a supportive atmosphere in which people of our particular sexual orientation are treated with respect. At Dartmouth, if not in society, let us put an end to beastophobia."

No, we didn't get recognition or funding. But we did make our point, and the point was well covered in the local media. The biggest paper in New Hampshire, the Manchester *Union Leader,* had a hilarious feature titled, "Students Go to the Dogs."

Another of our escapades involved the Indian symbol. Dartmouth had banned the Indian symbol as offensive to Indians. We sent out a survey to more than one hundred Indian tribes across the country. We included a picture of the Indian symbol and asked the tribes to decide whether they found it offensive. When we got the results back, we found that most tribes *loved* the symbol. The vast majority wanted

Dartmouth to retain it. Some tribes had even voted on the issue. When we published the results of our poll, there was a long silence in Hanover. The administration was so used to trotting out the head of the Native American Studies department, trusting that his views could be taken as representative of the Indian population. But we had demonstrated pretty conclusively that it was not so. *Fortune* magazine published an article on our exposé, and we were emboldened to try other stunts. One of them was to pay a local company to fly a plane over the field during Dartmouth football games. The plane dragged a huge banner that said GO DARTMOUTH INDIANS. The students cheered, and the administration was furious, but there was little the deans could do.

Our greatest success was undoubtedly the Cole incident. Professor William Cole was a black music professor who seems to have been hired to fulfill affirmative action requirements. He was given tenure despite his publication record, which was virtually nonexistent. His specialty was racial and political diatribes, which he delivered in class in a kind of street dialect, laced with obscenities. In short, Professor Cole was a God-given opportunity for the *Dartmouth Review.*

We sent a reporter to Cole's class during the first two weeks of the semester, in which students are allowed to audit courses and no attendance is taken. Our reporter taped Cole's diatribes, which appeared in the paper under the title "Bill Cole's Song and Dance Routine." Cole had described white students as "honkies" and women as "pussies," and he praised a man who had tried to blow up the Washington monument as an enlightened opponent of a racist society. The article produced a sensation on campus. This wasn't our opinion, these were direct quotations, and they were on tape.

The Dartmouth faculty rushed to Cole's defense. They passed a resolution denouncing the *Dartmouth Review,* the first of many, I might add. The faculty took the interesting position that they had full academic freedom to teach, and they accused us of tramping on that freedom. The officers of the *Dartmouth Review* responded by passing a resolution denouncing the Dartmouth faculty. We noted in our resolution that while they had the academic freedom to teach as they wished, we had the First Amendment right to criticize it.

Incensed by our article, Cole sued the *Dartmouth Review.* He claimed that his reputation had been trashed, which of course it had. He wanted several million dollars. The only problem with Cole's suit was that truth is a complete defense against libel. Cole never alleged that our article was inaccurate, only that it had shown him to be a fool. Our position was that he was, in fact, a fool. And the court apparently agreed, because it dismissed his lawsuit. Cole then turned to the Dartmouth administration for help. But what could they do? Disgusted, Cole resigned his tenured position at the college. The last I heard he had opened up a drum store somewhere in Vermont.

The Cole story, however, was not quite at an end. Cole's wife, Sarah Sully, who is white, was a tenured professor of French at Dartmouth. She assigned her class a paper in which students were asked to give their assessment of the *Dartmouth Review*. Most of the students knew that Sully was married to Cole, so, whatever their actual views, they submitted papers very critical of the conservative newspaper. But one student who didn't know who Sarah Sully was submitted a paper in French that said he enjoyed reading the *Dartmouth Review* and often agreed with it. When this student got his grade back, it was a C. He showed it to a few friends, and they suggested he go to the head of the department. The head of the department, a fair man, convened a committee of three professors who gave the paper a B. Sarah Sully was then asked to change the student's grade. She refused, and resigned her tenured position at the college.

As a consequence of its outrageous exploits, the *Dartmouth Review* became nationally famous. Of course we were regularly denounced by the *New York Times* and other publications. But our editors did appear in *Newsweek* and on ABC's *Nightline*. Our exploits were praised by conservative magazines and by the editorial page of the *Wall Street Journal*. Many Dartmouth alumni found out about the administration's misdoings through these national channels, and

Dartmouth's president was the chagrined recipient of many phone calls that began, "What the hell is going on up there?" Eventually the *Dartmouth Review*'s influence spread to other campuses. Inspired by our example, conservative students on some fifty other campuses started alternative newspapers. Many of these are still around, so that the spark we kindled has become an enduring flame.

Looking back at the *Dartmouth Review* with some perspective now, I see that it accomplished four major objectives. First, it trained a whole group of young conservatives in journalism and activism. Some of them have gone on to distinguished careers in politics. One of our editors, Peter Robinson, wrote Reagan's Berlin Wall speech, "Mr. Gorbachev, tear down this wall." Another, Laura Ingraham, is a regular pundit on radio and television. Ben Hart published a successful book about his Dartmouth exploits and now runs a large direct-mail company that raises funds for political candidates. Greg Fossedal wrote editorials for the *Wall Street Journal* before joining a money market research firm and settling down to father six kids. Keeney Jones wrote speeches for Bill Bennett and is now a Catholic priest. None of these people would have taken these pathways if they had not worked for the *Dartmouth Review.*

Second, the *Review* was, and remains, a valuable check on the excesses of the Dartmouth faculty and administration. Over the years the newspaper's exposés have forced the administration to abandon many a cherished liberal program. Who knows what other outrages the administration might have perpetrated had the *Review* not been around? As Professor Hart has said, thanks to the *Review,* "Dartmouth is no longer a place where the liberal sheep can graze unmolested."

Third, the newspaper generated lively discussion at Dartmouth about a whole slate of issues that would not otherwise have been talked about. Even the paper's critics admitted this. As the *New Republic* editorialized, "The *Dartmouth Review* has succeeded where countless tenured professors have failed," in fostering ongoing debates on campus about free speech, affirmative action, the liberal arts, and politics.

Finally, the *Review* moved the political center at Dartmouth decisively to the right. When I return to Dartmouth now and ask a typical student, "What are your politics?" the reply is, "Well, I'm a moderate conservative. I voted for Bush, but I am not as right-wing as those guys on the *Dartmouth Review.*" What this student does not recognize is that it is the influence of the *Dartmouth Review* over the years that enables him to say that. Moderate conservatism was totally outside the pale when the newspaper was founded. But by staking out a kind of far-right position, the *Review* has legitimized a wide range of positions in the middle.

After Dartmouth, a number of us headed to Washington, D.C., to be part of the Reagan revolution. (By this time I had given up on the idea of business school. Why learn how to market widgets when there was a fellow in Washington who was trying to change the world?) Amazingly, several of us ended up writing speeches for Reagan's cabinet secretaries, or in the White House. I had the thrill of working in the White House office of domestic policy. How exhilarating it was for us to see so many of our conservative principles put into practice, and to see them changing America and the world for the better.

When Reagan left office, I began my career as an author. My first book, *Illiberal Education*—perhaps the first book-length exposé of political correctness—was largely an extension of my Dartmouth experience, as I investigated the diversity revolution in academia and successfully employed my journalistic technique of embarrassing people by quoting them. My subsequent books have also benefited from my liberal education at Dartmouth and are all, in one way or another, explorations of the meaning of America. My latest book explores the relationship of the culture war to the war on terror. I continue to speak and debate regularly on the American campus, where my goal is to inspire the conservatives, persuade the moderates, and flummox and bewilder the left. What a great way to make a living!

Despite the conservative political gains of the past couple of decades, liberalism continues to dominate our culture. In fact, as liberals have been thrown out of office in Washington, they have retreated to the universities, the foundations, the philanthropic sector, and the media. Consequently, these institutions have moved further to the left. The conservative strategy that we used at Dartmouth—of seeking to subvert liberal culture by challenging its basic assumptions—is more relevant than ever, and it needs to be applied beyond the campus. Think of the rebel conservative media that have emerged to counter the monopoly once enjoyed by the major networks and influential newspapers like the *New York Times*. The right-wing media—such as the *Washington Times*, the *Wall Street Journal* editorial page, the Rush Limbaugh program, conservative talk radio, and the Fox News Channel—are consistently iconoclastic, irreverent, and entertaining. They reflect the *Dartmouth Review* model being applied on a national scale. We need more of this kind of spirited activism. I know about the obstacles, but even so, I wish more young conservatives today went into journalism, politics, and the academy, and fewer took the familiar path to business school and a career in banking or investments. How else are we going to change the culture? Besides, as I have discovered through my own career, harpooning liberals can be fun.

The *Dartmouth Review* recently celebrated its twenty-fifth anniversary, making it one of the longest-lasting independent campus newspapers in America. I hope it keeps going, and that the numerous other "alternative" publications on campus are also successful. I learned a lot at Dartmouth, and I consider my tenure at the *Dartmouth Review* to be central to my learning experience. In fact, the last time I got a call from my class agent reminding me of how much my Dartmouth education had benefited my career and asking me to contribute to my alma mater, I told him, "Bill, I already have. I sent a check last week to the *Dartmouth Review.*"

Down and Out
with Paul De Man

HEATHER MAC DONALD

Heather Mac Donald is a John M. Olin fellow at the Manhattan Institute and a contributing editor to *City Journal*. She is a recipient of the 2005 Bradley Prize for Outstanding Intellectual Achievement and author of *The Burden of Bad Ideas* (Ivan R. Dee, 2000) and *Are Cops Racist?* (Ivan R. Dee, 2003).

PAUL DE MAN was "deconstructing" Marcel Proust, and the graduate students in Yale University's Comparative Literature Department faced a dilemma. Here before them was the most influential literary theorist in America, one of the founders of an intellectual movement that had taken over the humanities nationwide. Yet were they to show the adulation that they felt for their renowned professor, they would betray the "mystifications" that de Manian deconstruction so ruthlessly skewered—belief in the reality of another human being, for example. And so the Comp. Lit. students, gathered in the sun-filled library of Yale's Linsley Chittenden tower that fall day in 1980, managed to continue projecting the world-weary sophistication that the cult of deconstruction required.

Paul de Man, for his part, was the very picture of rumpled humility. With his head hanging down and a chuckle periodically interrupting his soft European-accented speech, he could have been reciting a limerick on the British rail system. Instead, he was demonstrating that Proust's novel *Du côté de chez Swann* was bereft of meaning, contrary to the experience of countless enchanted readers. And as he proceeded through the predictable deconstructive hatchet job, a feeling of dread overcame me: "I never should have come back."

I was just awakening from a long spell. As an undergraduate at Yale in the 1970s, I had fallen under the thrall of deconstruction, a radical literary theory then emerging in Paris and in the United States, above all at Yale. Now, after two years of study in England, I was back in New Haven to start a Ph.D. under the professors I had revered in college. Except that this time around, something was wrong. Their utterances struck me as utterly mad.

My disillusionment with deconstruction was the moment I first realized how dangerous elite thinking can be and how seductive its ambience of chic leftism. That I had been sufficiently stupid to fall for it was galling enough. But I wasn't the only one. My professors preceded me, and they should have known better. What is more, they sent their acolytes into the world armed with the prestige of advanced thought, to become professors themselves and misguide the young.

In the years since, deconstruction has transformed the

study of the humanities everywhere. Whole departments in scores of universities have fallen under the sway of "Theory," a stylistically barbarous, philosophically frivolous mode of writing and thinking that reduces great art—indeed, all sorts of human achievement and historical fact—to arbitrary linguistic categories and oppressive power structures.

When a professor rants about the Bush administration's war crimes in an English class, he is taking his warrant from Theory's contempt for literature as such. The academic infatuation with race, class, and gender derives from the deconstructive obsession with "difference." It all amounts to a betrayal—of the humanities, of the students who wish to study them, of the university's mission. How did this happen? My own experience—the story of a nightmare from which I did, at last, awake—may offer a clue.

≫→

I arrived at Yale in 1974 just as the revolution was beginning. "Theories" were detonating around campus every day—poststructuralism, semiotics, Lacanian psychoanalytics. These mostly French imports—each giving off emanations of danger and taboo—purported to take up longstanding and important questions about how language works and how literature achieves its effects. Some even claimed an august philosophical genealogy through such European thinkers as Hegel, Husserl, and Nietzsche.

It is not worth tracing those alleged influences, however, because deconstruction and its sister theories reached conclusions so far outside any possible chain of reasoning that they make their philosophical forebears virtually irrelevant. These conclusions may be simply stated, for all the arcane jargon with which they are usually expressed: (1) There is nothing outside the text. (2) Because verbal signs are arbitrary—in principle, we could name a cat a "book" and a book a "cat"—words can never successfully convey meaning. (3) Human beings are merely epiphenomena of language; they do not otherwise exist.

Experience, of course, contradicts each of these claims every day. If a deconstructor's university were to suddenly stop paying his salary on the ground that he is, after all, just a verbal sign and thus not requiring of much upkeep, he would have his lawyer on the phone in less time than it takes to say "phallologocentrism." And he would expect his attorney to make legal arguments that would compel his university to start paying him again because those arguments would be 1, true, and 2, fully comprehensible.

But deconstruction's appeal lay not in its intellectual power—it had almost none—but in its aura of transgression. The eager uptake of deconstruction throughout the American academy marks the moment when universities gave up any pretense of being places of serious thought. Deconstructive prose reads like a cross between the Marquis de Sade and Attila the Hun. The year after I entered Yale, the once-respectable Yale French Studies published an extended meditation by French Theory guru Jean-Francois Lyotard on Theory as prostitution. The only parts of the essay that are remotely comprehensible are the dirty parts:

> "Penises, vaginas, asses, skins ought to be operated on so that Love should become the condition for orgasm." This is what the lover or the mistress dreams in order to escape the dreadful duplicity of the surfaces pervaded by the drives. But this operation would be an appropriation or propriation, as Derrida says, and ultimately a semiotic (system) in which erections and discharges would signal without fail the drive motions.

By the 1990s, colleges would start including real pornography in courses and conferences, but it could hardly match that original titillation of deconstructive prose.

With a Nietzschean self-infatuation, deconstruction's early followers felt themselves to be possessed of a dangerous new knowledge that only a favored few were sophisticated enough to embrace and that rendered the rest of the university's work nugatory. The graduate students ranked Yale's literature departments with as unforgiving an eye as a bouncer at the latest nightclub. The Comparative Literature and French departments, and much of the English department were in; the German and Spanish departments were pitiable backwaters that still believed in literature's ability to express the sorrows and joys of life.

Despite such departmental laggards, Yale was the place to be, and the chosen members of the deconstructive elite reveled in their prominence. No other university possessed as large a number of faculty members doing "Theory." Among the most well-known were Marjorie Garber, Barbara Johnson, and J. Hillis Miller—all of whom would later migrate and bring the deconstructive virus to their new campuses. Above them towered de Man, the soft-spoken Belgian scholar of Romanticism, whose slim output of increasingly bizarre essays belied the magnitude of his influence. He found himself eclipsed only once a year, when Jacques Derrida would arrive to deliver a talk.

Derrida's visits threw Yale into a frenzy of expectation. In the weeks before, his lecture topic—say "The Trace and Plato's Pharmakon"—would be posted in humanities offices across the campus. He arrived trailing yards of white scarf and draped in soft, elegant suits; professors seen walking with him as he tossed off French intellectualisms were instantly catapulted into the empyrean. He spoke before packed crowds in the high-ceilinged Comparative Literature library, lips pursed and hunched over his notes. His audience would sit rapt—I among them—through his signature obfuscations, wheel-spinning puns, and meaningless neologisms.

"It is because the proper names are already no longer proper names," he might say, "because their production is their obliteration, because the erasure and the imposition of the letter are originary, because they do not supervene upon a proper inscription; it is because the proper name has never been anything but the original myth of a transparent legibility present under the obliteration; it is because the proper name was never possible except through its functioning within a classification and therefore within a system of differences, within a writing retaining the traces of difference, that the interdict was possible, could come into play, and, when the time came, as we shall see, could be transgressed; transgressed, that is to say restored to the obliteration and the non-self-awareness at the origin."

When he was done, none present dared show his blank confusion. An ambitious graduate student might step up to the plate with a question:

Graduate student: "If the phallus always remains in place in the system of *la lettre*, where is the exterior of the exterior or the interior of the interior?"

Derrida: "What is veiled is a hole, a *non-étant*. Truth is 'woman' as veiled/unveiled castration. Nothingness is openness as a hole between the woman's legs." Audience members would recompose themselves into ever more portentous expressions of profound thought.

Plenty of my classmates dismissed deconstruction; I now regard them as preternaturally wise. At the time I scorned them as anti-intellectual. The conclusion is unavoidable: I must have lacked all common sense.

In high school, I had already decided that language was the most important and interesting thing on earth. Deconstruction's obsession with linguistic signs, then, seemed a perfect fit. I didn't notice, however, that its practitioners had a deaf ear for the beauty of words. Rather than reveling in verbal glory—like Melville's image of the White Whale "seen gliding at high noon through a dark blue sea, leaving a milky-way wake of creamy foam, all spangled with golden gleamings"—the Theorists would find a way of reducing it to a mute commentary on the failure of the sign. I sat through class after class in which this massacre-by-Theory was perpetrated on wonderful passages from Keats, Wordsworth, or Hölderlin. In retrospect, it is appalling; then, it seemed daring and exciting.

Though deconstruction's aura of being cutting-edge drew me in, my gullibility also illustrates the power of apparent learning over young minds. I had loved Yale at first sight because it seemed to embody the scholarly ideal. So if its hottest literature professors were answering the great questions of signification with a theory of linguistic breakdown, then the theory must have value. And the very difficulty of its prose seemed to prove it: Anything that hard must be good for you. I have wasted precious hours of my life in the stacks of Sterling Library struggling over just one essay of Jacques Derrida's—"La Mythologie Blanche"—time that should have been devoted to European history or Augustan literature.

And my lousy choices illustrated the problem: The university had abdicated its educational responsibility, leaving students to their worst instincts. If a brave soul from the Philosophy Department, say, ever stood up during one of Derrida's coy meanderings to challenge his misappropriation of Hegel, I do not recall it. And though some members of Yale's august faculty may have fought the march of Theory through the university (the heroic Donald Kagan comes to mind), they largely conducted their battles behind closed doors. Students rarely heard counterarguments to deconstruction's juvenile nihilism or learned why they would be better off sweating over Latin syntax and Gibbon than Michel Foucault and Julia Kristeva.

"The cognitive function resides in the language and not in the subject," de Man wrote. The text "knows and asserts that it will be misunderstood." No one ever asked de Man to explain in what way a text "knows" something if its putative author has no "cognitive function" whatsoever. De Man's later writing, slavishly imitated by his epigones, was inexplicably filled with images of mutilation, violence, and muteness, all ascribed to the most lovely poetic language. Analyzing Shelley's long poem "The Triumph of Life," de Man preposterously claimed to find the poet's dead and "defaced" body in the margins of the manuscript (Shelley had drowned before finishing the poem)—a "mutilated textual model," de Man wrote with typical sadistic relish, "[that] exposes the wound of a fracture that lies hidden in all texts." It is enough to make one long for the *Norton Anthology of English Literature.*

One of Paul de Man's star graduate students, Timothy Bahti, headed my literary theory discussion group. This chain-smoking, wiry-thin student of German Romanticism was totally committed to the de Manian project of exposing human life as a rhetorical fiction. In class, if anyone ventured the suggestion that human beings can actually communicate pretty darn well, Timothy Bahti would respond with a strangled laugh, his tongue poking ironically into his cheek.

Timothy Bahti's intense nihilism was charismatic. My book marginalia started imitating his microscopic script, whose near-invisibility was undoubtedly meant to shrink language into the muteness that de Man said was its natural condition. Following Timothy Bahti and de Man, I saw literature as one long meditation on itself. Every "text" seemed to refer to its own status as linguistic object, unable to control its interpretation or capture its referent. I wrote my senior thesis under the Wordsworth scholar Geoffrey Hartman. Hartman danced with the deconstructionists, but was not truly of them. A kind, elfin man whose face could jump instantaneously from sparkle to furrowed seriousness, he gleefully adopted the punning style then in vogue. Though he never came close to the unhinged nihilism of de Man, he never pushed me to think about Wordsworth without the crutch of deconstruction's apparatus, either. My thesis on "representation" in "The Prelude" was a flawless specimen of High Theory, in which I saw allegories of "reading" in such natural images as a snow-white ram reflected in a mountain pool.

Upon graduation, I could think of no greater good than a life of literary study, preferably back at Yale. I went first to Cambridge University, where I was known as *text qua text* for spouting deconstructive propaganda obsessively. But I also studied linguistics, which, unlike deconstruction, actually knows a thing or two about language. I became particularly smitten with speech-act theory, which delightfully presents words as active forces in creating social reality.

This knowledge proved subversive. When I returned to Yale in 1980 to begin a Ph.D. in Comparative Literature, I soon realized that the professors whom I had so worshipped had been for years mechanically repeating a fiction—and not a pleasant, uplifting fiction, at that, but a gratuitously perverse one. Deconstruction was a weird made-up story about language that had almost nothing to do with the real thing. A crisis of faith was looming. After just one semester in the graduate program, shaken in my belief system, I took a temporary leave of absence and never went back.

The reality of life outside the text eventually became my principal object of study, but I spent a while getting there. Theory cancer had colonized my mental DNA and would not release me for years. I decided to go to law school, not because I wanted to become a lawyer but because I wanted to continue studying hermeneutics. So naturally, I chose a law school as much like Yale's Comparative Literature department as possible. I enrolled at Stanford, where Critical Legal Studies, the Marxist-infused legal version of deconstruction, was running at full throttle.

I went through law school in a Theory-induced daze, unable to see that legal principles were pragmatic solutions to real-world disputes. Instead everything looked like a problem of language. Evidence was all about epistemology; the Uniform Commercial Code's Article Two, which governs contracts—in truth, a text of considerable elegance and seductiveness—was, for me, all about performative language. I wrote a law review note applying speech-act theory to the Code's Article Three, which governs promissory notes and other negotiable instruments. A nagging sensation that I was missing something rather crucial—that negotiable instruments met credit needs in a commercial economy and didn't just illustrate the problem of determining intent in an illocutionary utterance—led me to lose confidence and withdraw the note from publication.

I finished law school knowing less than I should have known about the law itself. Soon I was clerking for an appeals court judge. Meanwhile, an irony was engulfing the world of literary theory. Identity politics had invaded the university. The human subject had returned with a vengeance after having been banished by deconstruction. Theorists and their students started seeing literature as all about "me, me, me," defined exclusively in terms of their race, gender, and sexual orientation. And if they didn't see their particular color and gender of "me" reflected in a text or its author, then that text would have to go.

This infatuation with "identity" could not have been more antithetical to the deconstructive worldview, and yet, deconstruction's constant harping on "difference" had given rise to identity politics. The new multicultural literary theories retained all the rebarbative jargon of deconstruction, but put it to use pronouncing endlessly on the ways in which literature and society silence minorities, women, and homosexuals.

I watched with horror as the multicultural yahoos took over the humanities. For all its conceptual madness, deconstruction had at least been a mandarin science; it chose for its victim texts only the very greatest works of literature and philosophy. I feel extraordinarily lucky to have attended college in the 1970s, the last moment in which the canon was still intact. Amazingly, it had not yet occurred to anyone to complain that a syllabus contained only authors of the white male persuasion, so that is predominantly whom I read.

In 1987, Jesse Jackson arrived at Stanford University to lead the immortal chant: "Hey, hey, ho, ho, Western culture's got to go!" Student protesters claimed that Stanford's freshman year Western civilization requirement destroyed their fragile selves with the application of too many dead white males. Naturally, the university caved in to these adolescent know-nothings, who couldn't recognize a great piece of literature if it clobbered them in broad daylight. Cringing administrators replaced the Western culture requirement with something suitably multicultural, and the criterion of excellence in the selection of academic material was forever abolished. Every other university, faced with copycat protests by barely literate teenagers, sacrificed its precious cargo of masterpieces with equally cowardly alacrity.

In the same year, Paul de Man's collaborationist journalism was discovered. It turned out that he had contributed scores of cultural essays to Belgian pro-Nazi journals from 1940 to 1942. One essay argued that the Jews could be expatriated from Europe without any loss to European literature.

Oops! History and reality had intruded themselves into the airless world of deconstruction. Would its practitioners respond that the Holocaust was just a text? Yes, they would!

Rising in a universal snarl of rage against the press for daring to write about one of their own, the Theory establishment emitted a poisonous cloud of obfuscation that demonstrated what the world would look like if deconstruction's tenets were taken to heart: De Man was not responsible for his essays, because language always escapes the control of its users; the Holocaust was about the "impossibility of reading"; de Man's lifelong silence about his wartime writing was in fact a constant witnessing to the Holocaust, and an act of courage. In other words, ethical responsibility is a fiction and good and evil are completely interchangeable.

If anyone needed further proof of the dangers of such theory—not only to the study of the humanities but, one might say, to humanity itself—this was it. In my view, and contrary to deconstruction's gleeful critics at the time, de Man's journalism did not in itself discredit deconstruction. Too many others had contributed to the theory to reduce it to one man's past. The response of de Man's defenders, however, did forever disqualify the theory from any further claim on students' attention. I kept waiting for some Theory bigwig to express disgust at the apologists' moral autism. No one ever did. This was all the more depressing, given that deconstructive "insights" had embedded themselves in the culture at large.

Around this time, identity politics was paralyzing New York, where I now lived. The Tawana Brawley hoax, racially motivated boycotts of legitimate businesses, and anti-Semitic killings, all came out of Al Sharpton's masterful exploitation of the rhetoric of racial victimology. The city cowered before him. The poverty industry played the victim card as well, arguing that New York's massive welfare apparatus was necessary to overcome the legacy of racism.

Until this time, I had always been a liberal by default, the inevitable condition of those who do not bother to educate themselves about social facts. Unconsciously absorbing the received wisdom in the academy and the media, I had casually assumed that the rich oppressed the poor and that capitalism was unfair. When my Holdsworth bicycle was stolen from in front of the Yale law school, I felt that redistributionist justice had been done. The judge I had clerked for, Stephen Reinhardt of the U.S. Court of Appeals for the Ninth Circuit, was one of the most left-wing in the country. I found nothing amiss when he seized every opportunity to correct America's small-mindedness with his more generous liberal values.

My disillusionment with deconstruction had brought out my cultural conservatism; Al Sharpton's war on New York only increased my contempt for multiculturalism. As for politics outside of race, however, I remained a simpleton product of the dominant ideology. But when I started reporting on urban affairs for *City Journal,* I discovered that literary theory was not the only place where idiotic ideas eclipsed reality.

One of my early articles concerned New York's homeless advocacy industry. Liberal New Yorkers blamed "greed" for the vagrants who colonized Manhattan's streets. If only the city's plutocrats would support adequate shelter for the "homeless," this self-righteous line of thinking went, the problem would disappear. I talked to outreach workers and the "homeless" themselves and found quite a different reality: New York spent a huge amount on housing and services, but the "homeless" wouldn't bite. One program alone exhausted seven hundred thousand dollars in one year trying to persuade Times Square's disheveled street population to accept free apartments; only two vagrants out of hundreds took up the offer. The rest preferred the freedom of a homeless lifestyle, made possible by the city's numerous feeding programs and other giveaways (one charity even delivered hot pizza to vagrants' cardboard boxes). The "homeless" were still on the streets, I concluded, not because there was no housing for them but because the advocates needed them there to serve as symbols of capitalism's failure. Were the advocates ever to lose interest in dramatizing their socialist fantasies, the homeless would be removed to safer abodes and the city's streets returned to public use.

Soon I was writing about such topics as welfare, illegitimacy, and crime. To do so, I had to look at facts on the ground. I was talking to people who had been in jail or who felt threatened by those who should have been there. I sat in on police-community meetings in Harlem and rehabilitation sessions on Rikers Island. I visited high school day-care centers for the babies of ninth-grade students.

Over and over again I saw life contradicting the claims of official race and poverty ideology—the "Theory" outside the classroom. Far from being victims of society, the underclass poor, it seemed, had brought many of their problems

on themselves through self-destructive decisions—as they
would often acknowledge to me in conversation.

I heard scathing critiques of welfare from the recipi-
ents themselves—it makes you a zombie; people should
be required to work; women are staying at home all day
watching *Jerry Springer,* too apathetic even to change the
forty-watt light bulb in their apartment.

The welfare queen was not a figment of Ronald
Reagan's imagination; I met one at the county welfare office
in downtown Los Angeles: a tall woman in leopardskin
pants, stiletto heels, and fashionable sunglasses, renewing
her participation in the Supplemental Security Income
program, allegedly for severely disabled adults.

I encountered the entitlement mentality in the person
of Rhafel McElrath, who magnanimously allowed his girlfriend to support him from New York's generous welfare
program for able-bodied childless adults. (This chivalric behavior meant that she, not he, would have to do workfare.)
McElrath had submitted his own food stamp and housing
applications. "Let them pay my rent," he told me defiantly.
"I'm going for every dime I can get out of them." He had one
caveat, however: "If they make you work, I'm not doing it."

Conservatives had arrived at a critique of the social
welfare industry long before I was even aware that conservative social thought existed. When I began reporting,
I found myself retroactively corroborating their insights,

above all, about the importance of personal responsibility and a universal standard for behavior. I still don't start from a pre-existing theory about the state or the individual, however, though I often arrive at the same conclusions as a more rigorous conservative ideology. To the extent that conservatism tries to honor reality, I consider myself an adherent; when it attacks the Enlightenment or reason, however, I part ways.

I write on various forms of idiocy now—including the facile left-wing attacks on post-9/11 security measures, the knowledge-crushing banalities of "progressive education," or the charge that policing is shot through with racism. None of them are as tragic, in my view, as the idiocy that brought down the tradition of humanistic learning. The professoriate had been given the greatest luxury society can offer: studying beauty. All that they needed to do to justify that privilege was to help students see why they should fall on bended knee before Aeschylus, Mozart, or Tiepolo, in thanks for lifting us out of our usual stupidity and dullness. Instead, they set themselves up as more important than the literature and art that it was their duty to curate and created a tangle of antihumanistic nonsense that merely licensed students' ignorance.

If I could wish one successful campaign for conservatism, it would be to revive loving and humble scholarship. The ever-growing opulence of American life suggests that our political arrangements, while far from perfect, are re-markably effective in improving our material well-being. The denigration of high culture in the academy, however, is an unmitigated loss. With the great voices of the past stilled, our lives are so much poorer, no matter our freedom or wealth.

Pig Heads

STANLEY KURTZ

Stanley Kurtz, a senior fellow at the Ethics and Public Policy Center, is a contributing editor at *National Review Online* who writes widely on both foreign policy and "culture war" issues. His writings have also appeared in the *Weekly Standard,* the *Wall Street Journal, Policy Review,* and other publications. He received his Ph.D. in social anthropology from Harvard University and later taught at Harvard, winning several teaching awards for his work in a "Great Books" program. Kurtz was also Dewey Prize Lecturer in Psychology at the University of Chicago. His book, *All the Mothers Are One,* about family life and religion in India, was published by Columbia University Press.

THE PIG HEADS gave me my first inkling that there was something not quite kosher about the Vietnam-era left. I don't mean that metaphorically. I'm talking about actual severed pig heads impaled on poles carried by antiwar demonstrators in New York's Central Park. It was April 1969, I was fifteen, and my family happened to be touring New York City when we ran smack into half a million people staging the first big antiwar demonstration of the Nixon presidency.

To a precociously political teen, that demonstration was a dream come true. By the time I was fourteen, I was marching against the war in my hometown of Pittsburgh, Pennsylvania, and pounding the pavement of my suburban neighborhood for Eugene McCarthy's antiwar presidential campaign of 1968. I was rooting for the demonstrators when they were brutally beaten by police outside the 1968 Democratic National Convention. Reports that police had been provoked by demonstrators hurling bags of feces did bother me. And the 1968 takeover of campus buildings by students at Columbia University struck me as childish and stupid, an exchange of reasoned argument for sheer willfulness. Still, it took actually seeing those severed pig heads to give me a truly queasy feeling about the antiwar movement.

My initial inclination was to turn the pig business into a plus. How amazing is this movement that can accommodate Orthodox Jews, radical Palestinians . . . and pig heads! If that's not brotherhood, what is? Still, it was hard not to see those impaled pig heads as a warning to the police (in those days called pigs by demonstrators), and ultimately to all supporters of the war. "This is what we will do to you, pigs." Not quite kosher, this fifteen-year-old reluctantly concluded. Not that I was yet anywhere near turning right. My discomfort over those pig heads was merely the first small movement in a long, slow estrangement from the left.

I grew up liberal, but a liberal of a particular sort. My passion was for the free exchange of ideas and the power of fair debate. That sounds like pap, I know, or a perhaps pious projection backward from adulthood. Yet with all the nerdy

naïveté I could muster, I idolized the vision of liberalism pro-
pounded by John Stuart Mill. Let all sides freely offer their
best argument, and in the long run truth will out. Bad ideas
wilt under the pressure of intelligent criticism. At the time
I knew nothing of Mill. My model was the American Civil
Liberties Union, which, in 1969, courageously fought for the
right of the Ku Klux Klan to protest, even if that protest included the advocacy of violence. Eight years later, in 1977,
the ACLU defended the right of Nazis to parade through
Skokie, Illinois, a suburb where many Jewish survivors of
the Holocaust had settled.

The ACLU's defense of Nazis and Klansmen seemed to
me the height of political nobility (and I still admire it).
Nothing could be worse than these vicious anti-Semites. My
father's family had lost relatives in the Holocaust, and I'd
been profoundly affected by tales of the Holocaust's horrors.
That is exactly why the willingness to let Klansmen rail
against Jews and blacks, or Nazis freely march through a
town of Holocaust survivors, felt like ultimate tests of liberalism. I was moved by these heroic exercises in forbearance,
convinced that allowing bigots to freely air their noxious
views was the best way to fight them.

My liberalism was also shaped by my father's tales of
the fifties. Stunned by the Great Depression, Dad had been
infatuated with Marx in his youth. Later, the truth about
Stalin snapped my father out of his romantic socialism,
while the Holocaust, which Dad saw close-up as a soldier in

World War II, turned him Zionist. Yet my father remained quite liberal, and was an eager reader of left-leaning journalist I. F. Stone's famous *Weekly*. Dad told me that in the fifties, he'd had to get his *I. F. Stone's Weekly* delivered to someone else's apartment, for fear of retaliation by McCarthyites. Yet my anything-but-conservative father was addicted to William F. Buckley's TV show, *Firing Line*. We loved to watch the debates together.

So the Holocaust and McCarthyism were touchstones of evil. Yet as a child and teenager, I absorbed these lessons through the prism of a Millian liberalism, considering it my duty to encourage free debate, and to familiarize myself with the best arguments on all sides of contemporary issues. I collected my father's back copies of *I. F. Stone's Weekly,* read them thoroughly, and stored them in a little library of my own. But I also subscribed to the conservative *Human Events* to make sure I understood the other side. I was a charter subscriber to the liberal *Washington Monthly,* and later used the first edition of Michael Barone's *Almanac of American Politics* to memorize the Senate and much of the House. (Now that I'm a pundit, I have trouble keeping track of who's who.) And in a veritable apotheosis of adolescent nerdity, this sixteen-year-old was probably the only private citizen in the country with a subscription to that staple of libraries, *Vital Speeches of the Day.* I even made a point of visiting the local John Birch Society, just to chat with those appalling reactionaries and see what made them tick. (The more extreme Birchers had been cast out of the mainstream conservative movement by William F. Buckley in 1963.)

Although focused on the war, I was much inspired by the civil rights movement's achievement of racial integration through nonviolent protest. Even in 1964, when I was eleven, I remember being outraged that Goldwater had opposed the Civil Rights Act. I was a passionate supporter of Johnson in 1964. But when, in the late 1960s, I first heard about affirmative action, I was incredulous. I knew that in my father's day, quotas had kept Jews out of many fine schools. And I'd internalized the principle of reward for individual merit, not birth, that I took to be at the core of ACLU-style liberalism. So it shocked me that my father had no problem with affirmative action. And it rocked me far more deeply when, years later, the ACLU itself became one of the chief supporters of affirmative action. That was a decisive moment in my drift away from what liberalism had become. But in my teens, I could barely believe that affirmative action would catch on. I knew it was a betrayal of liberalism.

≫→

My first true political challenge came in October of 1969, six months after that demonstration in Central Park. I was a junior and a representative on my high school student coun-

cil. In ordinary circumstances, the proceedings of a high
school student council would be of little moment. But 1969
was no ordinary year.

Consider the emblematic example of blue jeans. I remember the very day that blue jeans could first be worn in
class. A couple of kids started wearing jeans to high school.
Our principal, Dr. Glenn (his and all other names in this essay are pseudonymous), got on the loudspeaker to announce
that blue jeans were inappropriate for school because they
"denote farm labor." Next day, half the high school showed
up in jeans. Dr. Glenn capitulated, and kids have been wearing jeans to school ever since.

So the principal (like other educators in authority during those years) had only tenuous control of our school. His
power came in for a serious test when the first truly national
antiwar demonstration was scheduled for October 15, 1969.
That was to be Moratorium Day, when opponents of the
war across the nation were supposed to take off from work,
demonstrate, and effectively shut the country down.

That was certainly Gordon's plan. Gordon was head of
our high school's chapter of the SDS (Students for a Democratic Society), the group that had organized that demonstration in Central Park. Gordon was the center of militance
on our student council. He wanted Dr. Glenn to shut down
the school on Moratorium Day, or he planned to force it
closed with a mass student walkout. To say the least,
Gordon's plan displeased Dr. Glenn. The principal threat-

ened serious punishment for Gordon, and for any student who walked out.

In a tense negotiating session in the principal's office, I positioned myself between Gordon and Dr. Glenn. I opposed the war, and wanted to honor Moratorium Day. Yet the idea of shutting down the school seemed wrong (a bit like those pig heads). What about students who supported the war? If they wanted to stay in school, who were we to stop them? In any case, we were obligated by law to be in school.

I suggested that we suspend classes for half a day and assemble the entire school in the auditorium, where we would stage a debate on the war. Gordon hated the idea, but Dr. Glenn reluctantly agreed, seeing it as the best way to avoid a walkout, and potentially serious trouble. I was thrilled. We'd honor Moratorium Day, give prowar students a fair shot, and do it all legally. I worked with the head of the fledgling student Republicans to invite speakers for a debate. Judging by student enthusiasm, it was a huge success. I took the experience as proof that liberalism as fair and open debate really could make social peace.

Gordon never forgave me, but I did get a reward. A few months after Moratorium Day, the school was again thrown into turmoil. Our newly elected student council president—the only student in my English class who'd been to Woodstock—was hauled into court on charges of being the biggest marijuana pusher in school. Dr. Glenn got on the loudspeaker and let us know that he was voiding the election re-

sults. The resulting uproar almost shut down the school
again. But my Moratorium work had been noticed, and I
was elected student council president on a platform that put
me midway between the principal and the radicals.

»→

By the time I entered Haverford College, in 1971, I was looking for a career in politics. I figured I'd major in political science, get a law degree, then just dive in. I remember being
taken aback freshman year when one of my poly-sci professors wore a political button to class. Although I'd never
thought about the issue, I had an immediate visceral sense
that this was wrong. A teacher's job is to offer his students
the fundamental alternatives and allow them to choose
for themselves. If anything, I thought, a teacher ought to
be mysterious about his political views. Many professors
still worked that way, but the politicized university was
emerging.

  Freshman year saw a bitter boycott of classes by Haverford's black students, some of whom had been admitted under affirmative action and were doing poorly in school. They
soon rebelled, accusing Haverford and everyone in it of racism. Like everyone else, I was pressured by left-leaning white
students to sign a petition acknowledging my racism. Many
signed, but I and some of my friends refused.

What bothered me most about the black student boycott was its chosen tactic. Haverford's blacks protested by remaining silent. They refused to discuss or debate, and instead insisted that white students engage in "consciousness-raising" until they'd discovered and acknowledged their own racism. This was a clear betrayal of the liberal commitment to open exchange, and I would have none of it.

The following year, after seeing an ad for what looked like an interesting lecture, I went to hear a guest speaker at Haverford's black student union, naïvely assuming I'd meet some of the white students who'd tried to get me to sign that petition. Instead I was amazed to find myself the only white student in attendance. The lecture turned out to be about the coming racial revolution. Questions focused on the precise nature and timing of the violence (i.e., which whites would be killed and when). I left dumbfounded. Pig heads indeed.

At one point, virtually everyone at Haverford collectively traveled to the capital to lobby against the war. We visited liberal Michigan congressman John Conyers, and heard a talk by the antiwar congressman Father Robert Drinan. The whole adventure was rather like the walkout that Gordon and the SDS had wanted back in high school. Only now, even the school administration was on Gordon's side. The fact that Haverford was a nominally Quaker institution, with a pacifist heritage, allowed a fig leaf of justification. Yet few of us were Quaker.

By rights I ought to have objected to the position in which this trip would put Haverford's few conservatives. Who would dare oppose the left-liberal consensus in class when the entire college had been expected to lobby for a Vietnam pullout? (Little did I realize, this was precisely the point.) But with the administration and the activists standing together, I sensed that objecting would turn me into a pariah. So I hid my concerns—ultimately, even from myself. After all, I was against the war personally, so it was easy to go along. Under social pressure, I was abandoning my principles and getting sucked into the vortex of what, fifteen years later, would be named "political correctness."

More important, my intellectual interests were drifting away from politics. I credit my first poly-sci class, where I read Plato's *Apology*. This hooked me on political philosophy, which directed me to a whole set of "meaning of life" questions seemingly distant from the carnival of everyday politics. Nietzsche's "death of God," Marx's theory of history, Weber's sociology of religion, Freud's unconscious, Plato's complex dialogues, and John Stuart Mill's defense of the liberalism I'd absorbed as a teen now preoccupied me.

So my interest in politics declined, but did not disappear. I never felt the hatred for Nixon that seemed to motivate so many. But despite my occasional qualms about the excesses of the left, I remained a committed liberal. Certainly, I supported George McGovern in 1972. And I was fascinated by the unfolding Watergate scandal. (Once a news

junkie, always a news junkie.) For a while, I was a member
of the student council and extremely active in Haverford's
internal politics.

Still, college is famous for provoking existential crises,
and mine was a doozy. I was preoccupied with the collapse
of religious faith (my own, and society's around me). And I
wanted to figure out if the social sciences (which had made
it hard for me to believe in anything) could tell us something
useful or positive about the human condition. This made
me a fellow traveler of the many nineteenth-century intellectuals who saw modernity's crisis of faith as a problem. It
also distinguished me from the emerging generation of
"postmodernists," who viewed religious decline as strictly a
cause for celebration.

Halfway through my junior year, I realized that politics was now my avocation, not my vocation. I decided not
to run for student council president and switched majors
from political science to religion. I wanted to be a scholar,
not a politician.

After a stint in a secular master's program in comparative
religion at Harvard Divinity School, I decided to seek a Ph.D.
in anthropology. That took me to graduate school at both
Harvard and U.C. Berkeley. I liked my fellow graduate stu-

dents, but sensed a gulf between their interests and mine. Many of these future professors were dissatisfied with their course work and attracted to various forms of Marxist or post-Marxist theory. They were blending their work with politics.

I'd turned from politics to a different set of issues, focusing my studies on the nexus of religion, psychology, and family life. These concerns had a long history within anthropology, yet were just then turning unfashionable. Years later, when Edward Said's "postcolonial theory" came to dominate the academy (championed by all those grad students who'd been attracted to Marxist theory), I was told that my wish to write about religion, psychology, and family life in non-Western cultures was a deplorable form of neocolonial oppression.

Yet it took more than the intellectual left to drive me right. The "real world" intervened as well. In the summer of 1979, just as I was moving from Cambridge to Berkeley, I took a three-week trip to the Soviet Union. I went with a detached anthropological curiosity and little political intention. But what I experienced shook me to the roots.

It started when the book I was reading (Hedrick Smith's *The Russians*) was confiscated at Moscow's airport. Intellectually, this was no surprise, but the reality of the event shocked me. The worst moment came when I inadvertently got a musician into trouble (how bad I don't know) just by giving him a pair of blue jeans and a rock music album. (Someone who'd seen us called in the police to question the musician.) Then, at a bookstore in Leningrad, the manager told me there were no Russian-English dictionaries in stock. On my way out, a clerk who'd overheard quietly slipped a tiny one into my palm without charge. After several such encounters, it became evident that ordinary Soviet citizens were continually being watched.

On a visit to Leningrad's ethnographic museum, I met a Soviet anthropologist specializing in Africa. It stunned me when I learned he'd never been permitted to visit Africa, and had no access to works on Africa by Western anthropologists (which he badly wanted). Yet I soon discovered that our tour guide (and translator) did have access to Western publications. She'd read Hedrick Smith's *The Russians,* and much else. Books that got confiscated from visitors like me were traded among the party intelligentsia. A decade later, these cosmopolitans were no doubt key supporters of Gorbachev's reforms. So both Soviet censorship and its unintended consequences were tributes to the revolutionary power of freely flowing opinion.

Although the Soviet subway system was awe-inspiring, the country's economic achievements were few. Nowhere was this more evident than in a failed Soviet version of Disneyland bravely named "The Exhibition of Economic Achievement." The Exhibition's colorful pavilions, filled with gigantic reproductions of newspaper articles about the latest barley harvest, lay deserted. Real Russians had trouble getting meat, yet nearly every meal with our tour group featured more beef than a normal person could eat. Our hosts had simply proven that they knew nothing of what an actual meat meal looked like. Restaurant service was pathetically bad. And why not? No one could be fired.

My visit to the Soviet Union put me in mind of those lessons about communist folly I'd been taught in sixth grade. Since then, attacks on the Soviet system had fallen out of fashion. Yet the most important lesson of my trip was that everything I learned about communism in sixth grade was right. Never was I so relieved as when I landed at Frankfort airport and set eyes on an American soldier.

≫→

Back at U.C. Berkeley, I strolled the plaza at lunchtime, listening to live rock music and watching students dressed in a thousand styles of blue jeans stuff themselves with meat at boutique-style cafeterias. I rolled my eyes at the omnipresent activists passing out Marxist literature. I couldn't forget that I might have gotten some poor Russian into trouble just for giving him a taste of what these kids took for granted.

Now this news junkie read the *New York Times* with changed eyes. Reagan, Reagan, it was always Ronald Reagan: James Reston, Tom Wicker, and the rest seemed to care more about Ronald Reagan's "evil empire" remark than about the reality of the Soviet Union. Against my own inclinations, I had to admit that Reagan was right. When the president was shot by an assassin early in his term, I heard people on campus cheering. Again those pig heads. Again my disgust.

When Reagan's U.N. ambassador, Jeanne Kirkpatrick, came to Berkeley to give a speech, demonstrators shouted her down. That was unsurprising, but it took me aback when even faculty members argued that Kirkpatrick ought to have been silenced. In the new enlightened view (a world away from the ACLU's stand in Skokie), oppressors had no free speech rights. Of course, calling Jeanne Kirkpatrick an oppressor was itself ridiculous. Kirkpatrick was a hero to Soviet dissidents, who hung on her every word. Yet here in Berkeley even faculty members deemed it noble to effectively confiscate Kirkpatrick's talk, as if they were airport censors in Moscow. As for me, I hadn't subscribed to *Vital Speeches of the Day* to buy into the idea of quashing a real live vital speech.

By the time I returned to Harvard to finish up my dissertation in 1986, affirmative action was pervasive. A teaching assistant confessed to me that he was giving his minority students inflated grades. When Harvard professor Harvey Mansfield got into trouble years later for claiming that affirmative action had played a role in grade inflation, I believed him. Moreover, with scientists still overwhelmingly male, colleges were turning to the humanities and social sciences to make up informal gender quotas for faculty appointments. In my field, where since Margaret Mead women have always had a presence, women were getting the good jobs. Men languished.

But the deeper effect of affirmative action was intellectual. Initially, affirmative action had been treated as a regrettable necessity: a temporary violation of individual rights for the sake of a greater good. But no one wants to think of himself as a temporary exception to proper academic standards. So the beneficiaries of liberal condescension became the carriers of a new ideology. The rise of academic postmodernism, with its assumption that classic democratic principles are just a cover for white, male, heterosexual, first-world power, is directly attributable to affirmative action. Precisely this sort of thinking leads to the notion that "oppressors have no free speech rights."

$$\gg\!\!\rightarrow$$

The dam burst in 1987 when I picked up a copy of Allan Bloom's *The Closing of the American Mind.* Thirteen pages into the book, I ran back to the store to buy an extra copy. Bloom began with the paradox of relativism: our certainty that truth is uncertain. Then Bloom connected this intellectual incoherence to our fragile families, the vacuity of popular culture, and the rise of what would shortly be named "political correctness." Soon I was deliberately purchasing copies from stores that served as feeders to the *New York Times* best-seller list. I'm convinced I took the book to number one. Regrettably, Bloom's executors have not seen fit to reward me.

Before Bloom's book, there was no "culture war." Bloom framed the issues, and in the process changed my life. *The Closing of the American Mind* gave voice to a thousand fugitive thoughts and feelings I'd only half-acknowledged for years. I gave the book away because I needed to know what others would say about these fundamental problems in the academy and society.

What a mistake. My naïve faith in open debate was clearly unsuited to what the American academy had become. In the anthropological world, Bloom was strictly taboo. Given the vitriol with which Bloom was excoriated by professors in my field and others, I soon realized that even mentioning him was a potential career killer. So for years I avoided joining the National Association of Scholars (NAS), the chief opponent of academic political correctness. When I finally threw caution to the wind (still carefully directing mailings to my home, not school), I discovered that my clever NAS chapter used envelopes with no external identification. I had to chuckle, remembering how my father had directed his *I. F. Stone's Weekly* to a decoy apartment. Now the trouble was coming from the left, and I was the one running scared. I'd turned right, all right—right into a political train wreck.

Teaching in a "great books" program at Harvard in the midnineties, I found myself embroiled in a running controversy over the curriculum. Left-leaning teachers had pared back assignments from the great books and substituted a series of contemporary writings by neo-Marxists, postmodernists, and radical feminists. I didn't try to cut those writings, but I did seek (with little success) to add material from contemporary conservative thinkers. One day, while chatting with colleagues, we told stories of what we'd done in the sixties. On hearing my tale of Gordon, Dr. Glenn, and the Moratorium, my colleagues identified with Gordon: "Yeah, back in the sixties, we SDS types had plenty of experience dealing with pesky old-fashioned 'liberals' like you."

That's when I knew the inmates had well and truly taken over the asylum. Thirty years later, I was still trying to stage a fair debate in the school auditorium. But Gordon and his cohorts were in charge now, and what used to be called liberal was now excoriated as conservative. In retrospect, I could see that I'd absorbed that old-fashioned liberal ethos at the very last moment before it went into eclipse. That classical version of liberalism had served as the internal compass by which I'd navigated the shoals of academic political correctness.

Even so, I'd been effectively silenced. Alone, I couldn't balance the curriculum, or even safely commit my ideas to paper. The food, clothing, and music in elite universities were a whole lot nicer than in the Soviet Union, but the intellectual setting was barely better. I'd been preaching freedom of speech, but I had to leave the academy for the world of policy think tanks before I'd ever get a chance to practice it.

Being out of the academy transformed my life. For the first time in years, I could speak my mind. Yet by the time I escaped, the ethos of those elite campuses had migrated to the larger culture. Issues and attitudes long incubated in the universities now dominate the activist base of the Democratic Party. Secularism, antiwar sentiment, near hatred for religion, and disdain for convention: All of these were and are cultivated in the academy, and spread from there through society at large.

Like Justice Samuel A. Alito, whose conservatism was formed in reaction to sixties-era Princeton, today's conservatives—this one included—are increasingly shaped by their years in the academy. By virtue of its one-sidedness and extremism, the academy serves as a key generator of our polarized political and cultural battles. It would take a return of fair and open debate, and of the old-fashioned liberal values that make this possible, to give us a shot at social peace. Trouble is, Gordon's pals have all got tenure.

The Events Leading Up to My Execution

JOSEPH BOTTUM

Joseph Bottum is the editor of *First Things,* the nation's largest circulation monthly journal of religion and public life. His books include *The Fall & Other Poems* and *The Pius War.*

THE FUNNY THING is—but, really, there's nothing funny about conservatives. Grim, dour people. Humorless and gray. They spend their days moaning to one another in antiphonal chant about the evils of liberalism, and they wear white sweat socks—the old kind, with the two red bands at the ankle, that always had its elastic stretch so it drooped and puddled around your shoes.

I remember those socks. I wore them nearly every day the summer I was twelve, only with blue bands instead of red, and a pair of beat-up sneakers with a hole in the toe. Actually, now that I think about it, most of the time we just kicked off our shoes and socks, tying the laces together to drape them around our necks like fetishes of some deep Amazonian tribe. Even our summer-hardened bare feet would burn on the hot tar, and we'd balance our way down the street's long, straight lines of cooler paint or play a game of giant steps, in which the dashes of the broken white stripes were safe islands and the dark tar a bottomless deep.

But, um, conservatives. Yes. The laughless antifun, antifestival, antifreedom types. You've met them, of course: meddlesome maiden aunts scrawling *Killjoy Was Here!* on the walls of the pleasure dome while the rest of us are trying to get on with our orgy.

As it happens, my generation wasn't supposed to have such retrograde characters in it. The America in which we were schooled instilled in its children only two great commandments: *Be Nice,* and *Be Cool.* As for *Love thy neighbor and thy God*—well, sure, if you really want. *Eat your spinach and wear clean underwear*—a little Victorian, maybe, though probably not bad advice. But, above all, you must be nice, and you must be cool: nice, 'cause it's nice to be nice, and cool, 'cause, like, you know, cool people are just so *cool.* Quite how we were to go about combining, say, Albert Schweitzer and Lou Reed remains a mystery—but in any event, we knew that conservatives didn't have it.

So, one day around 1983, I'm sitting in the smoking lounge of the Georgetown University library—remember when college libraries still had smoking rooms?—reading *Tom Jones* (education is nice, our teachers had told us) while tendrils from my Marlboro (cigarettes are cool, the movies had shown us) spiraled up in blue-gray swirls to break and pool on the stained acoustic tiles of the ceiling. And, growing tired at last of young Tom's long journey to reconcile with Squire Allworthy and the all-too-worthy Sophia, I let my eyes drift to the window.

Down on the sidewalk, across the street, was a woman with a toddler in a baby stroller and a small black dog on a bright red leash. April is Washington's best month, and the sun filtered in a glow through the leaves of the new-green trees as the overexcited, overhappy little dog bounced and yapped, weaving his tangled leash through the stroller's wheels while the mother stumbled after him and the toddler laughed and laughed, clapping her small hands at the slapstick world into which God and her parents had unexpectedly delivered her.

I wish that words could fully re-create that scene—the sharp blue of the stroller, the mother in her red jacket straining for the dog as her snarled purse spilled coins and baby wipes across the brick sidewalk—for it was at that moment I began to fail at the great American goal of niceness and coolness at which I had been aimed since grade school. And it all started with the sudden, absolute conviction that babies are good.

No thought exists in isolation. One conviction leads to another, too fast sometimes to follow, and I stood there remembering in a mad rush all the college girls I knew who had abortions. I stood there at the library window, on that green April day, remembering all my complicity in joining the great sexual revolution that was supposed to empower women but mostly ended up empowering college boys to enjoy free and apparently consequenceless sex. And I knew that, fun as the pleasure dome had been, I must leave—for it was kept bright and warm with the bodies of aborted babies, burned in the basement furnace for fuel.

Maybe it wasn't quite that sudden. Even on the road to Damascus, a conversion proves to have been years in preparation—and to require even more years of learning the unintended consequences, before you find yourself sitting in a room with William F. Buckley and the Republican National Committee, not quite sure how you got there.

Besides, there are other natural conservatisms built into life, and thinking too much about any of them tends to drag one forward, like a prisoner being jockeyed up the steps of the scaffold. Language, for instance, has always seemed to me to have something inherently conservative deep down in the way it works; it preserves old words, old senses, and old commitments, and when you fall in love with the way words go together, you necessarily open yourself to the old ways of understanding the world. And then there's memory, the backward-casting struggle to keep alive those precise spots of time—the genuine feeling of balancing barefoot down the lines of reflective paint on a hot street, the true epiphany of watching a mother with her laughing child.

But real conservatism usually begins when you find in yourself a limit, a place beyond which you will not go, and always for me it comes back to this touchstone: Anything that participates in the murder of a child—anything that slices it into pieces or burns it to death with chemicals in the womb—is *wrong*. All the rest is just a working out of the details.

This truth comes at a cost: It cuts us off from the never-quite-achieved dream of niceness and coolness. There's a kind of outer darkness that envelops those who lost the all-American aspirations on which we were brought up. I mean, it's just not nice, and certainly looks uncool. Indeed, for more than a few of my earliest friends, it seems as though I have committed some great crime that ought to see me dangling from the nearest gallows—dressed, like all the other condemned conservatives, in those droopy white socks with the thin red bands at the ankle.

≫→

Still, a single limit, a single stand, is not a political philosophy, and there's a reasonable question of what American conservatives could possibly be trying to conserve. Indeed, if opposition to abortion were primarily a sentiment—a political feeling untethered from any system of political thought—it probably wouldn't be conservative at all. It would be instead something more radical than the nation has seen since John Brown saddled his horse and rode down to raise an army from the slaves around Harper's Ferry.

Fortunately, the modern pro-life movement in the United States is not dominated by its radical *sentiment,* in the political sense of the word. Its commitments are both far more profound and far more mundane than all that: a philosophical belief in the dignity of the human person asserted by Western civilization and approximately embodied in the American experiment, on the one hand, and a practical association with mostly Republican politicians, on the other hand.

I guess that's conservative. Certainly it is connected to what passes in the United States for conservatism, and if you work in the pro-life cause, you find yourself before long attending meetings with think-tank libertarians, and business advocates, and neoconservative foreign-policy analysts, and newly elected Republican congressmen without much clue of what they ought to stand for—except, of course, for re-election.

The trouble really is that we've never had any conservatism in the United States—at least, if we use "conservatism" in the strict European sense of the word: the preservation of the ancien régime, a government of throne and altar, and a perpetual endowment of medieval privileges for certain families, guilds, and classes. A nation born in revolution doesn't get to appeal to the traditions that it found so revolting. If we are conserving anything in America, it is the Revolution of 1776 and the Constitution's great 1789 experiment in freedom: an essentially anticonservative moment in human history.

Still, the American version of conservatism is trying to conserve *something*—and the best way to describe it may be as a balance between the Bible and the Enlightenment. You could argue, I suppose, that America is necessarily something like a Christian nation. You could argue, a lot more successfully, that the country's survival requires the continuing presence of the Judeo-Christian worldview from which it was born. But that's not quite the same thing as saying America must remain in good part a biblical nation. Language is a deeply conservative thing, and inescapably written through America's folk songs and revival-meeting calls and spirituals and political rhetoric are the cadences and the images of the King James Bible.

It is worth remembering just how stern that biblical language can be: "Think not that I am come to send peace on earth," Christ declares in the Gospel of Matthew. "I came not to send peace, but a sword. For I am come to set a man at variance against his father, and the daughter against her mother, and the daughter in law against her mother in law. And a man's foes shall be they of his own household."

The Bible is full of hard sayings like this—too many, too hard, to be entirely explained away in historical criticism, or eased with gentler passages in antidote, or shrugged off as the typical overstatement of all those wild-eyed, locust-eating prophets. From Genesis to the Book of Revelation, there is something all through the Bible that has no patience for political compromise, or moral casuistry, or conventional prudence, or philosophical judiciousness. It's not the only thing in the Bible, of course, but without it, we have no Bible. "A fire is kindled in mine anger," as Deuteronomy puts it, "and shall burn unto the lowest hell, and shall consume the earth with her increase, and set on fire the foundations of the mountains."

There is something in the United States, as well, that has always burned against the world. From Cotton Mather to William Lloyd Garrison, from John Brown to Martin Luther King, there has been a hunger here to speak with lips touched by burning coals, a blessed rage for the apocalyptic lessons taught only by tongues of fire. A nation formed by political geniuses—masters of compromise, philosophers of prudence, judges of wisdom—we are also a nation with another theme. Something here has, from the beginning, disdained political order and sought not to be brilliant, wise, and learned, but only *true,* though the heavens fall as a result. "I am come to send fire on the earth," Christ says in the Gospel of Luke, "and what will I, if it be already kindled?" It's not the only thing in America, of course, but without it there is no America.

This is a problem for politics. Indeed, it is the root of the theopolitical problem that haunts us to this day. The radical secularists—with their determination to strip the public square of all references to religion—began their long march through the nation's universities and law schools in the 1930s and 1940s, and they now wield considerable power.

But I have the sense, insofar as one can judge the tides of such things, that the secularists have lost the intellectual part of the battle and are running now only on the fumes of their irrational belief in antibelief. There is something quaint about them, some throwback to the days people boasted of being "freethinkers." That marvelously dated word fits them, and they seem, as a result, very much beside the point. It will take generations to undo the damage they did, and in the meantime there will be much to rage about in their sneers and stratagems. But hasn't the actual intellectual discussion of America left them behind? It's hard to name many serious political thinkers who haven't come around to admitting to some degree the usefulness and unavoidability of public religion.

Once we set aside the superannuated secularists, however, there remains the genuine theopolitical problem they masked from us for decades. Public order in a democracy—the structure of liberalism that needs a people of virtue to maintain itself—seems to require the bulk of citizens to believe in God. But no one ever believed in God for the sake of public order in a democracy. Especially not Americans.

A momentous dilemma results from this. Liberalism needs religion, and needs it in a variety of ways, from the simple genealogy of modernity's birth out of the spirit of Christendom to the complex reliance of modern times on a perduring set of premodern assumptions and virtues. But religion doesn't need liberalism, and the rhetoric of biblical prophecy would burn the world to the ground if a still, small voice demanded it. "God gave Noah the rainbow for a sign," as the old slaves' spiritual put it: "No more water, but the fire next time." And to reap the benefits it needs, a democracy must allow religion to remain the potential trump, the threatened uncontrollable, the possible authority outside a modern state that longs to have no authority outside itself.

Liberal democracy can be menaced even when the prophet doesn't return from the wilderness to preach fire and brimstone in the public square. Throughout our history, biblical America has often stood outside political America: the wayfaring stranger far away from the public man, however much the political world echoes with the words of a public God. And this, too, is a threat—perhaps even a greater threat than an abolitionist prophet like William Lloyd Garrison publicly calling the Constitution "a covenant with death and an agreement with Hell"—for it leaves us with a mass of citizens who suffer the political order merely because it doesn't occur to them to think it particularly important either to attack or to defend. "When ye shall see the abomination of desolation, spoken of by Daniel the prophet, standing where it ought not (let him that readeth understand), then let them that be in Judaea flee to the mountains."

In other words, the Bible may help produce the ethics a modern state needs to assume in its citizens if it is to allow them freedom, but the Bible didn't start out as the ethics of liberal democracy. It may not even contain an ethics at all, in the sense in which philosophers speak of "ethics."

There's a curious moment in the *Confessions* in which St. Augustine writes that he could find many religious truths in the books of the philosophers. He could find that in the beginning was the Word. He could find that the Word was with God, and that the Word was God, and even that by the Word were all things made. But one truth he couldn't find in the philosophers was that the Word became flesh and dwelt among us. This may not seem a great difference: If we admit the metaphysical necessity of the Divine at the highest level of human philosophical thought, then it seems not much more to allow that God might occasionally concern Himself with human affairs. But, Augustine concludes, this is the truth that turns everything upside down, for if God acts directly and willfully in human affairs, then He has broken history over His knee—choosing the foolish things of the world to confound the wise and the weak things to confound the mighty.

And where, in any of this, is there room to speak of

ethics? Render unto Caesar the things that are Caesar's, yes. Understand that God has allowed the sword to remain in the hands of the magistrate, indeed. But the day may come when a prophet is told to enter the public square and cast down the nations—just as the day may come when a private man is told, "Take now thy son, thine only son Isaac, whom thou lovest, and get thee into the land of Moriah; and offer him there for a burnt offering." And with these possibilities, ethics in any philosophical sense has disappeared. Whatever political benefits a state gains from biblical religion, how can a liberal democracy allow even the chance of such things? They are *immoral* on their face—or *amoral,* or *supermoral,* or *extramoral,* or use what word you will: They are outside the capacity of any ethical political order to allow.

Except that if the political order doesn't admit their possibility, then the political benefits of religion cannot be held, and democracy itself decays. "Whatever may be conceded to the influence of refined education on minds of peculiar structure," Washington famously warned in his Farewell Address, "reason and experience both forbid us to expect that national morality can prevail in exclusion of religious principle." The United States as it naturally wants to be—what we might call the platonic ideal of America—contains a tension we must be careful not to resolve. From its founding, the nation has always been something like a school of Enlightenment rationalists aswim in an ocean of Christian faith. And how shall the fish hate the water wherein they live? Or the water hate the fish?

Well, perhaps the last few generations of secularists showed us that it was possible. They would have been left gasping to death on the beach, had they ever fully succeeded, but genuine secularism—of the kind that would lead, for example, to French *laïcité* and the complete banning of religion from public life—was never really what the American political tension was about. In its modern form, that secularism was an import from nineteenth-century France and Germany, mostly, based on a notion of intellectuals' vast superiority to vulgar religious belief and a reading of history as proving that battles among Christian sects are the greatest danger to political order.

None of America's founders had a comparable disdain for religious belief, and American history contains nothing analogous to the European wars over Protestantism. Both sides "read the same Bible, and pray to the same God, and each invokes his aid against the other," Lincoln said of America's most costly division, and as the Civil War went on, his cadences and his thought grew more biblical, not less, as though only the language of the prophets was sufficient to express the horror and the necessity of the conflict: "Fondly do we hope—fervently do we pray—that this mighty scourge of war may speedily pass away. Yet, if

God wills that it continue until all the wealth piled by the bondsman's two hundred and fifty years of unrequited toil shall be sunk, and until every drop of blood drawn by the lash shall be paid by another drawn with the sword, as was said three thousand years ago, so still it must be said, 'The judgments of the Lord are true and righteous altogether.' "

No, the question in America was always how to reap the benefit from biblical religion while minimizing the dangers of extrapolitical authority and a set of citizens called by their deepest beliefs away from any desire to help defend the political order. Part of the American situation in the eighteenth century was historical accident, or perhaps—as Madison put it in an extraordinary letter—God's direct providence that preserved the New World undiscovered by Europeans until they were ready to try this experiment in freedom. But, whether the participants willed it or not, the American Revolution occurred in a Christian moment, formed most immediately by the progress of religion from the Puritans to the Great Awakening.

That gave the Founding Fathers massive advantages. From Max Weber's sociological descriptions to the economic analysis of John Paul II's *Centesimus Annus,* from the political thought of St. Augustine to the Christian realism of Reinhold Niebuhr, innumerable arguments have suggested that biblical religion offers enormous public benefits. And the examples of Maimonides and Thomas Aquinas make it impossible to deny that a philosophically sophisticated ethics can be reconciled with the superadded truths of biblical revelation.

But the overwhelming Christian faith of America also presented the Founders with terrible disadvantages, for the Bible cannot be entirely tamed to any public purpose or ethical reading. "Have ye not known? have ye not heard? hath it not been told you from the beginning? have ye not understood from the foundations of the earth? It is He that sitteth upon the circle of the earth, and the inhabitants thereof are as grasshoppers; that stretcheth out the heavens as a curtain, and spreadeth them out as a tent to dwell in: That bringeth the princes to nothing; He maketh the judges of the earth as vanity."

The tense and awkward solution of the Constitution derives, I think, from an awareness that the benefits and the dangers have the same root. "Biblical America" is the oxymoron that defines us, the contradiction that maintains us. If we lose either our extrapublic religion or our Enlightenment use of public religion—if we break the delicately poised balance between the force of Christianity and the drive of modernity, if either side in this tension ever entirely vanquishes the other—the United States will cease to be much of anything at all.

»→

The funny thing is—but, really, apart from the droopy socks, there's nothing funny about conservatives. You reject the great American dream of being simultaneously nice and cool, and all your friends begin to back away. The lady with the dulcimer closes her eyes in holy dread, and inside the pleasure dome, that miracle of rare device, they start to barricade the doors against you.

And maybe they're right, for, in its way, the schooling with which we grew up is an attempt to balance the same elements that created this nation. Niceness is what's left over when you keep the feeling of Christianity but forget its purpose, like St. Francis of Assisi—only without the faith. And coolness is what remains when you keep the mood of enlightenment but mislay its reason, like Voltaire—only without the intelligence.

But . . . but, there was the laughing toddler and her mother on the brick sidewalk in Georgetown. Years later, as I held my daughter—an infant of the newborn size at which they fit in one hand—I had a sudden vision of what it would mean to have aborted her: to have made her cease to be. And I handed her back to my wife and ran upstairs to vomit.

From such moments, there is no going back. Every step that leads from there to conservatism is like climbing the stairs of a scaffold. In the end, however, I'll take my Bible and my Enlightenment the way the American Founding de-

livered them: neat, not watered down to niceness and coolness. Of course, much of the time that makes me feel as
though I have mounted a rickety gallows—with the trap-
door of social rejection creaking underneath my feet. But
what other choice is there?

Pacifists, Pacifiers, and Snakeskin Miniskirts

DANIELLE CRITTENDEN

Danielle Crittenden is the author of the nonfiction book
What Our Mothers Didn't Tell Us and the novel *Amanda Bright
@ Home*. Her essays have appeared in the *Wall Street Journal*,
the *New York Times*, the *Washington Post*, the *Weekly Standard*,
and *National Review Online*, among other publications. She
writes a regular blog for the *Huffington Post*.

SO WEN DO oo tink oo can get ome?" My nose is stuffed up and my head feels as if a construction crew with buzzsaws has gone to work inside it. I'm lying facedown on a playroom floor with a ten-month-old baby boy crawling around and a three-year-old girl astride my back. The portable phone is pressed to my ear.

"I'll get there as soon as I can," my husband's voice says. "I'm so sorry you're so sick."

"So mm I."

"Let's play Belle again!" my daughter cries merrily. "You be Philippe [the horse]!"

"Cud we pleeth play sumpin elth?"

"No!"

"Pleeth???"

She emits a noble sigh and dismounts. Shoots of pain

run up and down my muscles. What time is it—my God, it's only one o'clock! Lunchtime seems like hours ago. How much longer can I do this? It's almost the baby's nap time. A wicked, fuzzy thought: What is the maximum number of videos a toddler can sit through without permanently damaging her brain?

"Let's draw pictures now."

"Don't oo wanna watch a moothie?"

"Draw."

". . . wif mommy?" I plead. "Mommy ith THO thick. Mommy needth to retht."

My daughter takes a moment to consider this. "Okay," she replies reasonably. "*After* we draw . . ."

»→

How on earth did I get here?

It's a question I'd ask myself often when my kids were young. Alternately: *What would my younger self think if she could see me like this?* Both thoughts were accompanied by a face-grabbing motion.

Frankly, I can't even imagine what my younger self would think of my now forty-three-year-old self, with *three* children, two dogs, one cat, and a somewhat dented minivan. Possibly something similar to the lyrics of the pop song

"1985" that my kids, for a time, insisted on blasting over the car stereo. It was about an SUV-driving, Prozac-popping middle-aged mom named Debbie, recalling the days when she had dreams—and a snakeskin miniskirt.

> *She was going to be an actress, she was going to be a star*
> *She was going to shake her ass on the hood of White*
>   *Snake's car!*

"Mom, did you have a snakeskin miniskirt?" This from the front seat, where my eldest daughter, now much beyond her "Belle" years, cocks a carefully plucked eyebrow at me.

I was twenty-two in 1985. I had a closetful of miniskirts. While I didn't dream of shaking my ass on White Snake's car, I wouldn't have had a problem with it. I did once stage a one-woman protest in a male-only country club and had to be carried out like a suffragette, except that it was all uproariously fun, and a bunch of us went out for drinks afterward . . .

"Not a snakeskin one."

"But you had a miniskirt?"

I'm not sure where my daughter's interrogation is heading: Is she asking me this because she wants to wear a miniskirt, and I have (hypocritically!) forbidden it, or because it is an amusing bit of maternal anthropology? Mom. Miniskirt. ROFL.

"Um, I think so," I say vaguely. "I can't really remember."

These days I claim not to remember a great deal of my early twenties—also known as the period of my life Before I Met Your Father. This seems to be a necessary parental strategy, one not so dissimilar from the one employed by Bill Clinton when he appeared in front of a grand jury. I find I'm constantly engaged, as the former president's critics put it, "in an effort to hinder, impede, and deflect possible inquiry." The daughter who once cheerfully accepted the Disneyfication of my marriage ("So after I grew up, I met your father, we fell in love and had a beautiful wedding") now asks ever more precise, subtle, and probing questions about my past. In reply, I find myself murmuring a lot of "Hmms?" and "Let me think about that and get back to you," and of course, the all-purpose "I don't recall." And I *know* I'm not the only parent my age doing this. My husband once observed that his high school class of 1978 may well have been "the worst high school class since the invention of high school." No class before or after has ever had less homework, more grade inflation, less supervision, more permissiveness, a lower drinking age, or a higher tolerance for teenage misbehavior.

Yet it didn't mean that all of us were wild-eyed liberals, either. I grew up in Toronto with a stepfather who'd traveled the world as a foreign correspondent for one of the local dailies, and who, during the 1960s, served as the newspaper's Moscow correspondent. He often entertained my brothers and me with funny—if unsettling—stories about the lengths he had to go through to buy common items, like windshield wipers and toilet paper, or about his phone being bugged by inept Soviet bureaucrats (whose coughing he'd hear on the tapped line). As I grew older, I found it hard to identify with the anti-Americanism that prevailed in Canada: I didn't understand those friends of mine who were more suspicious of the United States than of the Soviet Union; or who criticized American military actions in Nicaragua and El Salvador while ignoring the human rights abuses and enslaving of millions under communism. By the time I hit my twenties, I was a card-carrying member of the Reagan and Thatcher youth movements. If you'd stopped me on the street and asked me my views on privatizing the steel industry or pointing ballistic warheads at the Soviets, I would have given you unequivocally conservative answers (two thumbs up for both).

But—and this is a big but—as to my personal life, I'd completely absorbed the feminism of the 1970s. Its messages and teachings infused the culture I grew up in—so much so that my ideas about what I could do or the ways I could act as a woman didn't even register in my mind as being especially political. And to the degree they did, they did not seem to contradict my political views. Indeed, the conservatism of that era seemed to perfectly complement the feminist ideal of self-realization: It was exciting, forward-looking, spirited—a force that celebrated freedom and human potential and stood up to the deadening forces of socialism. It expressed the same optimism about the future that my girlfriends and I felt about being women. Just give us the opportunities—we will take them!

I remember sitting with my best friend in one of the new espresso bars that had just opened downtown. As my friend and I played with cappuccino froth and flirted safely with the thin, saucy man who took our orders (openly gay waiters arrived in Toronto at about the same time as espresso did), our futures felt gloriously open—and so completely within our own powers. There was no blueprint on the table. We'd spend hour after hour discussing all the possibilities of who we would be, what we would do, and all the different men we would love.

Looking back, I think we had some awareness that we were possibly the first generation of women to approach the workforce as a completely open oyster, and marriage and children as "choices" that we might or might not make eventually—but we did not in any way identify ourselves as feminists. We drew little connection between the dreams we expressed to each other and the newsreels of hairy, placard-waving women marching down Fifth Avenue that we'd watched as little girls. To a young woman in 1985, those "libbers" might as well have been blue-stockings in lace-up boots.

And yet, underlying our banal confidences would be assumptions and ambitions that would delight even the most fearsome of those libbers. Of course we were going to get jobs! Or rather, of course we were going to "have careers!" We wouldn't need a man to support us. No way! Ditto for marriage. My friend and I came from divorced families. Our mothers worked at jobs out of necessity—but they also enjoyed them. While it was strongly expected that we would earn a living for ourselves, very little had been expressed to us in the way of romantic expectations. Erica Jong's *Fear of Flying* was a worn paperback in the public library by the time I was old enough to read it. Her celebration of female sexual bravado and promiscuity no longer shocked conventional middle-class morality. The magazines we read for guidance on how to apply blush and eye powder offered relationship advice that assumed men were equally short-term as the season's new lip colors. Even our own mothers seemed to regard marriage as something similar to the onset of arthritis or some other age-related affliction: It would come upon us soon enough, and we should try to pack in as much fun and experience as possible before we were crippled by it.

Leaning over our coffees, my friend and I would assure each other that we would never become one of "those"

women. There was no need to spell out who "those" women were. We didn't know many of them, but the few we'd met over the course of our childhoods scared us to death: the dreaded "homemakers" who still went through the motions of keeping up the appearance of a family long after their husbands had walked out and their eldest children opted to become stoneheads in the basement; mothers who had sunk all their time (and dreams and identities) into raising their daughters, only to have those daughters regard their sacrifice with scorn or indifference. They were like the Ghosts of Womanhood Future to those of us who might heedlessly "sell out" and get married.

One of my first jobs was working the night shift in a newsroom answering the phones. After dinner all the crazies would start calling in—the spaceship spotters, the readers who were sure the government was beaming messages into their brains, the wives trapped at home with toddlers. The last group sounded the most out of their minds. They'd want to speak to their husbands, who were, in some cases, working until two in the morning. I could hear the weariness in their voices as kids screeched and jumped in the background. I'd put the call through to Dad—some otherwise tough beat reporter or city desk editor who'd lower his voice and coo a goodnight into the receiver.

Pathetic! I'd think. Never was I going to be one of those women on the other end of the phone, waiting for my husband to get home while squirrely toddlers used me as a human jungle gym. Never . . . !

»→

Um, okay. Fast forward.

I began to question my feminist assumptions when, as a reporter in my early twenties, I began to cover press conferences and marches held by local women's groups. At first I was enthusiastic. I knew the movement had moved on from its libber days, and I was keen to see where it was and where it was going. I'd show up, notebook in hand, ready to jot down positive quotes and further the cause, whatever it was. After the first few assignments I grew discouraged. I'm not quite sure who or what I expected it at these events, but it was not women I met: gaggles of extreme radicals protesting everything from mascara-testing on rabbits to cruise-missile testing in the Arctic; grim-faced lawyers and politicians in bow-tied power suits, bemoaning the "glass ceiling" and demanding government-imposed "pay equity" programs (which were not any easier to understand when they called them "equal pay for work of equal value" programs, and, either way, seemed more suspicious than the "equal pay for equal work" expectation of the generation before). Unfailingly, these activists would claim to represent the interests and opinion of the "majority" of Canadian women. Pretty soon I got balky and began to ask them questions: Would the "majority" really agree that American cruise-missile testing was the number-one issue facing women in the country? Did "the majority" really want every single job in the economy recategorized by sex, with wages to be determined and set by a new bureaucracy?

One day I followed a dubious group of protestors into the main intersection of the financial district and watched as they laid their bodies down in front of traffic. Their point was to "end male capitalist oppression of women" but all they managed to do was bewilder and amuse the passersby—the "majority" of them working women enjoying the sun on their lunch hour.

And it was not just the politics of these activists that bothered me (although of course that was part of it: Why did sticking up for women mean, de facto, that you had to subscribe to socialist policies?). It was more their constant assertions of victim status. I'd read the rah-rah essays of Gloria Steinem and Betty Friedan. Sisterhood was supposed to be powerful—not whiny. *Just give us our opportunities—we will take them!* And yet here were female lawyers—some of them the most powerful women in the country, leading lives their grandmothers couldn't have even imagined—complaining about their status. Or rallies of angry, alienated female activists blaming men for everything: nuclear power, the free market, Western literature, and so on.

A couple of things were going on, of course, that I didn't realize at the time. First, the very success of the 1970s women's movement meant that those protesters who stuck with it, long after its original demands had been realized and its ideas absorbed into the popular culture, tended to belong to the radical fringe. Mainstream followers didn't feel the need to show up at rallies, so what was left were protesters who simply adapted their crude Marxist worldview to a feminist one, swapping the word "man" for "imperialist." But second and more important, a new wave of academic and political thought was forming to counter the very problems that had come with success—and that is what those lawyers and politicians were beginning to articulate in their demands for pay equity. What happens when you do grant women the same opportunities as men—but they decline to take them? Are there fewer women CEOs because of sexism, or a system that is inherently sexist—or because women, for reasons of children and family, differ from men in their ambitions, and shy away from such demanding and all-consuming career paths?

These issues had only just begun to be debated (I learned early on as a reporter that to even raise them opened you up to enormous criticism: In 1987, I wrote a magazine cover story about the emerging battle between working and stay-at-home mothers. The subsequent "Letters to the Editor" page was illustrated with a copy of the magazine lit on fire). But these "new" feminists—who would later be called "difference" feminists—were grappling with both the success and the failure of the "we're-all-just-the-same-as-men" theory of the early movement. Success, because women like me were indeed building our lives upon feminist assumptions; failure, because it clearly wasn't working. Women *were* different, and those differences had consquences. Women still bore the babies, so we also bore the choice of abortion or single motherhood in a culture that encouraged casual sex and discouraged male commitment. Women still took the lower-paying jobs, because they were still by and large the ones raising children—and so we were more likely to be left struggling and poor in an era of easy, no-fault divorce. Therefore, according to these difference feminists, the entire economic, legal, and social structure had to be changed in order to make it more "fair" for women to . . . be women.

The difference feminists often unfortunately expressed a crazy hostility to men—and a spinsterish dread of the male sex drive. It's thanks to them that companies were forced to pay out millions of dollars in legal settlements because somebody made the wrong kind of joke over the water cooler. And it's thanks to them that so many young, confident women were put off by their wince-making brand of feminism. Girl, get a life.

But still, the difference ladies were on to something. It

was just something that I and many of my peers didn't want to hear. What I didn't understand—and tragically, many young women still fail to understand—was that my seemingly modest and reasonable expection for an exciting, productive, and happy life as a woman actually amounted to the grandest and most complex demand in the history of the human species. Yet the only way I was going to find this out was by trial and error. As I mentioned, there was no blueprint: Each of us setting out on adulthood back then was invited to create our own "rules." While it seemed liberating, a girl could waste a lot of years discovering some very basic truths. Or discovering them too late: such as, it's much harder to meet a man after thirty, and harder still to get pregnant after forty.

Obvious, maybe, but not obvious then—not when everyone you trusted told you to the contrary. Do it your way! But frankly, a society that tells young people they must all write their own rules is a society that is asking young people to do more than all but a small minority of people are able to do. We do not tell young people they can't have a house before they learn how to be architects, carpenters, and plumbers. So why do we tell them that in order to have a successful marriage and family life they have to devise their own system of moral philosophy?

And yet, even as my generation works its way through the false promises of feminism—even as it makes its peace with the costs of delaying marriage and childbirth, with the difficulties of reconciling the work-home dilemma ("mommy wars"), with the terrors of infertility and marital instability—we continue passing on false messages to the young women who come after us. I still find that one of the easiest ways to offend female students in a college audience is to suggest that their list of "goals" should be headed by marriage and motherhood—even if, or especially if, marriage and motherhood are what they ultimately desire. We continue to maintain the illusion that we are entirely self-sufficient creatures whose destiny is fully in our own hands. That illusion doesn't hold up so well when you meet the man whose destiny you wish to share—and shatters entirely when you become responsible for the destinies of new people whom you have given life.

My own teacher, in the end, was raw practical experience. I ended up meeting the man I would marry at the then-shocking age of twenty-four. Four years later I would give birth to my first child. On both occasions I felt like I was succumbing to some freakish, retro-vision of womanhood. (Me. In a big white dress. ROFL.) "But you're so young!" was the general reaction of my friends to my "happy" announcements. My husband and I often felt absolutely on our own—like Renaissance Italians trying to figure out how to do things by looking at pictures and sculptures from a thousand years before. We debated everything we did, from the trivial (who should clear, who should load the dishwasher) to the profound (whose life would be most changed by the arrival of a baby). I look back on our early years of marriage as an intense series of labor negotiations and legal arguments eventually leading to a settlement. Hardly the Disney prince hoisting me up on his white horse, and so on. But happy, in the end.

And yet, for all our hard bargaining, all that we did was to work our way back to wisdom that had been accepted and followed for generations until our own: Hey, you know what? It does make sense that I stay home with the kids since a) your chest has no mammary glands, b) I don't trust you to take the baby out without forgetting it somewhere, and, more compellingly, c) *because that's the arrangement we both shamefacedly prefer.* Of course we put modern spin on it—I'm an "at-home mother" as opposed to the "housewife" of yore—but we have embraced a traditional model, in this as in dozens of other aspects of our lives. And I can't help noticing that many women of my generation—even those who would reject traditionalism in their politics—are finding their way back to these old personal truths as well. As I wait in the car-pool line, I see bumper stickers for John Kerry, John Edwards, and Howard Dean adhered to the other minivans and SUVs; through the rolled-down windows I hear more NPR than Rush. We may have taken different routes to get here, but we've arrived at the same place. Indeed, we're on our way to the next destination.

The "Debbies" in my circle of women are now leaving the world of young children and coming out the other end.

Some were once lawyers or executives. For a long period they were full-time mothers. As their children have gone into school, some have resumed their old careers, part- or full-time as their circumstances allow; others have come up with entirely new "careers" for themselves, volunteering at their children's schools or other community organizations. And some, without apology, have decided they would rather stay full-time mothers—with all the personal and financial risks inherent in the role.

What we share is the recognition that our old beliefs about marriage and motherhood were as much a product of our time as our miniskirts and Meg Ryan perms. We share the belief that we are in some sense together pioneers, who have gotten to this stage in life by slipping and fumbling our way along.

But if we have done anything, it may be to have come up with a new set of blueprints—something to hand to our daughters. They need them as much as we did—maybe more urgently, for the choices facing them are even more vast. They can reject them, of course. What they can't reject is the example so many women have now set: You can be an ambitious, and even very accomplished, woman and still reap the joys of motherhood and family. Your dreams don't have to go out the door like Debbie's—and whatever the song may say, I don't think the real Debbies' dreams did either.

Choices and Consequences

TOD LINDBERG

Tod Lindberg is a research fellow at the Hoover Institution, Stanford University. He is editor of *Policy Review,* Hoover's Washington, D.C.–based bimonthly journal, and author of *The Political Teachings of Jesus* (Regan Books/HarperCollins, April 2007). He writes a weekly column about politics for the *Washington Times* and is a contributing editor to the *Weekly Standard.* He is the editor of *Beyond Paradise and Power: Europe, America and the Future of a Troubled Partnership* (Routledge, 2005).

A S MY WIFE, friends, and colleagues will attest, I hated turning forty. At the time, February 2000, I thought it had something to do with fleeting youth—midlife crisis as one's arrival at the inflection point between the cradle and the grave. Cure: none. Known palliatives: Category Three, mistress, Everest expedition; Category Two, affair, sports car; Category One, subscriber internet websites, golf.

But it wasn't really fleeting youth or visions of mortality. I think the forty problem, rather, is about facing the notion that the gap between *becoming* who you are and *being* who you are is finite and rapidly closing. What comes into view around that age is the realization that the world is not one of infinite possibilities; that by one's own choices one has decisively foreclosed certain avenues; and that the net effect is rapid convergence on a person one had not yet met or even imagined the existence of: oneself. One will be spending the rest of one's life with this self; if all goes well, *as* this self—unalienated, that is, from the person one has become and the world one inhabits. But he arrives uninvited.

I don't mean to suggest that a life characterized by an awareness of forgone possibilities is necessarily melancholic. Whether it is would seem to depend on the nature of the possibilities forgone; surely it's good, not bad, to have shut the door on bad options, including some that were fun at the time. To pick a relatively safe example of naughtiness from a broad menu of possible citations, I have quit smoking, am happy to have done so, have no intention of resuming, yet can muster no real regret for having taken up the practice in the first place.

More seriously, one could say that the essence of mortal being and free will is to make choices that foreclose possibilities. Immortals do not have this problem: In an infinite amount of time, everything that can happen will happen; every binary choice resolved one way will present itself again for resolution the other way. There would be no *being* at the end of *becoming,* and so the passage of time would amount to no more than a bad infinity of essentially meaningless experiences. Not a cheery thought, that.

The alternative, however—a world in which people forgo the impossible for themselves by making choices—may turn out not to be so bad. The real test is the person emerging at the end. No, I will never conduct a symphony orchestra, nor play Hamlet. One's confrontation with these facts begins with the appearance on the scene of the figure of *who one is*—real but still distant, visible in silhouette but not in detail. And for me, at least, it was disconcerting. Who is that guy? Where did he come from? What does he want?

I don't have much use for assigning myself an ideological label these days. I don't mind being called a conservative or a neoconservative, except by people who don't understand that an important strain of modern "conservative" thought is nothing other than classically liberal thought. But there are, broadly speaking, two tendencies in answering the question of who you are, and by extension who others are; one is broadly "left" in political orientation, the other broadly "right."

The first is to ascribe the events of your life and the lives of others mainly to circumstances beyond your control: life lived imprisoned in the false consciousness of the oppressed proletariat, for example, or as the injured psyche produced by a broken home—or for that matter as the undeserving beneficiary by dint of fortunate conception of good looks, brains, and money. Now, no one really believes this in its radical form, just as no one embraces the comparably radical approach from the right, namely, that one is and must be master in all respects of one's fate, a kind of superman in the rank-ordering of human types. But the serious conservative alternative to the view that *in general* circumstance drives us to become who we are is the view that whatever circumstances may be, even quite awful circumstances, they never fully obliterate the human capacity to make consequential choices for better or for worse.

I think that's correct. So, that figure drawing closer and beckoning to me, what does he want? For me to take my share of responsibility for who I am.

⟫→

I recall two quite specific childhood anxieties: The first was that I would become a criminal. The second was that one day, I would lose control of my car.

It's hard to say which of the two was more upsetting to contemplate. On the criminal side, the question was how could I, a reasonably well-mannered only child from a loving family, end up so horribly on the wrong side of the law? How could I be driven to a life of crime, eventually to be caught and go to prison? Or perhaps even the electric chair? What possible sequence of events could come before me and produce such an outcome? The world had lots of criminals. They were all once children. For whatever reason, the life path of the criminal appeared before them and they set out upon it, only to come to a nefarious end. How awful that would be: the humiliation of going to prison for one's crimes, the disgrace one would visit upon one's family.

On the other hand, to lose control of one's car: In this case, I have a vivid recollection of the source of this anxiety: sitting in the passenger seat of the car, Mom or Dad driving, the AM radio on, the newscaster describing a crash in which someone died after having "lost control of the car." Here I was, riding in the passenger seat or stretched out in the back with my blue blanket on the way to my grandparents' house, feeling generally safe and happy, Mom or Dad driving, apparently fully competent at the task and at ease. And then, another one of those news bulletins. What was it about cars that caused people to lose control of them? To me, cars seemed very predictable, yet clearly, they were not. Otherwise, how could they wrest control from their drivers? Apparently, or at least so it seemed from all the radio reports of car crashes, this could happen to anyone, more or less at any time.

It's not hard to see where the problem lies here. I didn't really understand that the question of whether to be a criminal—to rob and kidnap and murder on the way to an untimely death in the electric chair—was actually up to me and no one else. Nor did I understand that in the normal course of events, cars do not deprive people of the power to control them. Barring catastrophic mechanical failure, when people lose control, it is generally their own fault. Your fate, at least in part, is something you make for yourself.

I can't remember exactly when I sorted this out. Certainly before I became a teenager. Around the age of eleven, I had settled on an ambition: I would become a lawyer. A friend of my aunt Marge's had introduced me to the wonders of the law: "Look around you—negligence everywhere, as far as the eye can see." "How about that person crossing the street outside the crosswalk," I asked, "is that negligence?" "It sure is." The perspective was illuminating. Suddenly, from a world of blamelessness in which the cruel fate of a life of crime was thrust without warning upon the innocent, and in which cars took away control from their drivers, I found myself in a world in which everyone was at fault for something if only you looked closely enough. This would, of course, include oneself.

But wait. What's the difference between the two worlds? In the first case, a cruel fate grabs you by the scruff of the neck and drags you to your doom. In the second, your awareness of the internal demons of your own deficiencies leaves you defenseless against the charge that whatever bad happens to you it is simultaneously beyond your control and your own fault, as the ill that finds others is theirs. And I suppose that if good things come your way, there is no other way to view them except as the happy accidents of a temporary condition that the negligence of mankind will sooner or later disrupt.

≫→

I had a recurring dream during my teenage years and on into my early twenties. It was that my mother had come back.

She died when I was thirteen. Possibly fourteen. It was summer. August. Sometime around the twenty-third or twenty-fourth. She had stomach cancer, at first misdiagnosed as an ulcer. I think she might have lived about three months after the doctors got the disease right. She died at home, in bed, on a Sunday. My father and I were out for a drive. My grandmother was at home. When we got back, the priest was there. Or maybe he had been there and left. He left mass early to come right over, they said.

During the final weeks of her life, once it was clear that the chemotherapy was useless, I adopted the ambition to make sure that the last words I said to her were "I love you." And I think they were, though I can't say for sure.

OK, I give up. What do you tell a thirteen-year-old (or a fourteen-year-old) by way of explanation for the fact that Mom is dead? I can't even remember what anybody tried.

The scar tissue here is rather thick, and that's the way I like it. I don't pick at it. I leave it alone. I didn't appreciate it when others caused me to take note of it as the scar tissue was forming, even when their purpose was to express sympathy. It is no small thing to be a bit vague on the question of how old you were when your mother died. It takes a certain determination. A lot needs forgetting.

One day many years later, after Dad and I said a final good-bye at the vet's to our family dog, Otto—who had per-

manently ingratiated himself with my mother by burrow-
ing into the side pocket of the short fur coat she was wearing
when we went to see about the dachshund puppy for sale—
we stopped for several weepy scotches at the Tally Ho, Dad's
main bar. We even managed to discuss our ability to cry over
the dog but not over Mom.

The dream: I am at home, and there's Mom! There she
is in the kitchen, sometimes making dinner. She's back. I
thought she was dead, but there she is. Great! But she isn't
saying anything. Where has she been? Why did I think she
was dead if she had just gone away for a while? Why *had*
she gone away for a while? Leaving me to think she was
dead? What kind of mom would go away for a while without any explanation, leaving the impression she was dead?
That's mean. Mom wouldn't do that.

Ah, right, no, she wouldn't. She *is* dead. This is not
really Mom. This is a dream about Mom. A dream in which
the pure joy of the return of Mom is fatally disrupted by the
incomprehensibility of a figure capable of generating such
joy by coming back ever having gone away in the first place.
The emergence of this paradox in the dream always woke
me up.

I would have to say that I woke up relieved. What are
the contortions through which one has put oneself in order
to wake up relieved that one's mother is, after all, dead? It's
enough to make you think fate grabs you willy-nilly by the
nape of the neck and does with you as it pleases.

»→

Downside: no Mom. Upside: complete freedom.

Dad didn't care what I did so long as—well, I don't know. If there were, as the diplomats say, red lines, apparently I didn't cross them.

My house was the clubhouse. Usually, it was a boys' club, but girls were always welcome. The editor of this volume is the author of a book called *Home-Alone America,* which describes the trouble kids are prone to get themselves into when left to fend for themselves unsupervised. Exactly. Who needs the backseat of a car when a room is available? Dad did become vexed once when he found evidence that people had been using *his* room. But in truth, a man of infinite generosity and bonhomie, Dad was more interested in the ongoing opportunity the incident afforded for teasing the male perpetrator.

I always thought of myself as an underachiever. I took German in high school, but I couldn't possibly have been bothered actually to learn the language with any degree of fluency. This sense of self lingers, no doubt because it is accurate. I am both a journalist who can't touch-type and a scholar without a Ph.D. I lack discipline as such as well as *a* discipline.

One day near the end of the second quarter of my sophomore year in high school—my worst period of what would today be called "slacking" and the only time I was at risk (not great) of taking a seriously wrong turn—my honors English teacher took me aside as I was walking by her classroom. Somewhat dazed for a variety of reasons, I found her overture unnerving—at the time, one would have said I was feeling "paranoid." An expression of solemnity on her face (her features, but not her expression that day, reminded me of my mother's), she informed me that under the percentile criterion by which she graded the class, I had not made an A—and that she had therefore decided to regrade the class on a curve because she thought I *ought* to have an A. Astonished, I thanked her much, awash in the edgy pleasure that attaches to getting away with something you shouldn't.

I was a Boy Scout; needless to say, I didn't make Eagle. There was something (I can't remember what) that I considered offensive in the requirements for the "Citizenship in the Community" merit badge, so I couldn't be bothered. Dad, an Eagle Scout himself, was disappointed. But our troop, which was under the leadership of my gang of neighborhood cronies, and was accordingly organized around the requirements of our permanent, floating nickel-ante, quarter-limit poker game, had an absolutely uncanny knack for winning every single competition at every single campout and jamboree we attended. Orienteering, bridge-building, watermelon-eating: We won them all.

One day at summer camp, we got mad at the junior

members of the troop for something, possibly waking us up too early, and to punish them we made them thoroughly police the area, tie up the tent flaps, and stow away their gear. Just as they finished, the inspectors came through. At the closing bonfire, we came away with the tomahawk for cleanest campsite.

≫→

I used to have long hair. At its longest, it was just about armpit length. There's a picture of me and the boys from a Scout canoe trip we took along the Minnesota-Canada border. When my daughters saw it, they wanted to know which one was Dad and who the girl was. Their mother explained that the girl was no girl, but in fact, Dad.

I cut my hair back to a seventies-respectable length my senior year of high school. By then, my band, "Hot Flash"—our compromise choice for a name after we had considered and rejected "Butt Funk"—had broken up (I was the bass player). More to the point, however, one winter day at my perch at the office of the Glenbard East *Echo*—in another exception to the rule, I had been the surprise choice of the outgoing editorial board for editor, having risen through the features section, not the news pages—I got a press release advertising the upcoming school board election. It specified the qualifications for office. You had to be a resident of the school district; eighteen years of age; and a citizen of the United States. *I could do that,* I thought to myself. So why not?

The district had four schools, Glenbards North, South, East, and West, and about eight thousand students in grades nine through twelve. There were two vacancies that year on the seven-person board and five people running. All the seats were at-large. You could vote for one or two people.

We wanted to come in second, behind the woman who was clearly the outstanding candidate in the field (and would become a good friend). She had the influential endorsements of both the teachers' union and the quasi-official "nominating committee," which had sent out the press release that got me going. They both also endorsed the man I needed to beat, a Ph.D. chemist working for a big oil company. His main interest in the position seemed to me not so much secondary education as bolstering his community-service corporate bona fides. I was the only one who was surprised that I didn't pick up either of the key endorsements; I was offended, especially at the absence of vision on the part of the teachers' union, but I forgave them on the strength of their failure to appreciate that I was going to win.

We ran a carefully thought-out campaign. As it happened, at the time, most of the members of the board came from the territory of Glenbards West and South. The only member from East was leaving the board, and I was the only candidate from there. I sought her out and obtained her endorsement. In my town, therefore, the flyer we distributed claimed "Lombard Needs Tod Lindberg," the implicit point being that even an eighteen-year-old representative is better than no representative. For the other areas, a generic flyer stressed my precocious achievements, such as they were, and my commitment to educational excellence. Our objective, therefore, was a big win in the East and not to provoke a backlash in the West and South. We would leave the North alone; we figured the two candidates from that area would split the vote there.

The biggest disagreement I had with Dad, who was de facto campaign manager, was over the "youth vote." He saw high school seniors who had turned eighteen as a potentially rich source of votes in a generally low-turnout election and wanted me to do outreach to them districtwide. I said I would but never did. In truth, I thought it was a bad idea. In the first place, it overestimated my appeal among eighteen-year-olds: I had a good shot at the school board running against adults, but I would have had no chance whatsoever at Homecoming king, class president, or anything for which you needed a package of such mass-appeal qualities as good looks, excellence in sports, and normal tastes and proclivities. In the second place, pitching an appeal to eighteen-year-olds would have offended my vanity. To the extent I was seeking validation, it was of my place at the grown-ups' table. Third, such a move, it struck me, might well create the very backlash we were trying to avoid. And in the fourth place, I didn't think I needed to do it to win; let us not forget that at this point in my young life, I had internalized the principle that the objective was not to try your hardest, but to achieve the result you sought.

On election night at district headquarters, when the Glenbard East returns came in overwhelmingly in my favor, we knew we were in. And although I have never chosen to try to repeat the experience, there really is nothing quite like the kick you get from winning an election.

The most immediate effect of my decision was to sharply curtail my college options: I had a three-year term to serve, later extended six months when the state moved school board elections to the general November ballot. I wasn't about to resign my seat five months after winning it to go off to college someplace else. I needed to be within reasonable commuting range of home in order to attend meetings two or three times a month.

Since my high school girlfriend was going to Northwestern and I didn't wish either to chase her or to appear to be doing so, I decided that the only answer was the University of Chicago. The decision to go to Chicago was easier, not harder, because of the reputation of the place as a haven for brainy misfits. Having by this time given up on my ambition to be a lawyer, I was especially impressed by the statistics the admissions people brandished about the high percentage of University of Chicago graduates who went on to get Ph.D.s. "Professor" might be good. Some type of writer, in any case.

I found myself in the fall of 1978 in a dorm room diagonally across the hall from a young man who was by lengths quite the most exotic character I had ever run across. Jewish, a New Yorker, voluble, witty, quick, brilliant—what uptight, middle-class, Midwestern suburban schoolboy had ever seen the like? He had, moreover, a story to tell of a world that, from about the moment I first heard of it, took hold of my imagination as the place I wanted to be. The young man was John Podhoretz, and the world he described was that of the New York intellectuals—the wing of which his family belonged to was then coming into national prominence under the rubric of a term I had never heard before, the "neoconservatives."

It's important to understand the origins of the "neoconservatives" as a subset of the "New York intellectuals." The circle of the parents of my college friend and subsequent roommate were both. The point is that the pedigree of neoconservatism traces back into an intellectual world that was distinctly not conservative. Anticommunist, yes. But procapitalist, surely not, and alienated from the mainstream of American society, surely yes. This was not the world of

F. A. Hayek, Russell Kirk, Willmoore Kendall, and William F. Buckley, Jr. Rather, its eminences were such distinctly odd-ball radicals, political theorists, and social, literary, and art critics as Dwight Macdonald, Harold Rosenberg, Clement Greenberg, Hannah Arendt, Daniel Bell, Irving Kristol, and Norman Podhoretz. The last two were figures of special fascination for me, because they were editors of publications that had brought out the best and most interesting writing I had ever seen. It's one thing to be the editor of your high school newspaper and to extrapolate from that to a possible career in the newspaper business; it's something entirely different to discover the world of the "little" magazine, in which brilliant people bandied about ideas with robust incisiveness and great wit. This was news to me—very good news.

As for the "neoconservative" aspect, there was a sense in which I could present myself as an instance of the classic profile of someone who moved from left to right, if you construe the long hair and pattern of seventies-era misbehavior in conjunction with uninformed but occasionally radical political views and a contrarian sensibility born of the desire to demonstrate how clever one is. But let's face it, this was a stretch. I was never a socialist. I ran for the school board on a platform of *increasing* graduation requirements because high school was asking *too little* of students. More basically, I was interested in a piece of *running* the school district, not of adopting toward it the posture of, say, a critical theorist.

Personal history aside, however, the then-dazzlingly fresh ideas associated with this, the heyday of neoconservatism, were hugely attractive for their insights into a world that seemed drastically out of whack—and, of course, included among these ideas was a vigorous critique of other ways of thinking about the world, especially those of the left. I found these arguments compelling. Was it necessary to acquiesce in the forward march of totalitarian ideology in the world? It was not. Was capitalism no more morally defensible, finally, than any other system based on favoring the interests of the wealthy and powerful? It was more defensible. Was bourgeois man, he of sober judgment and respectable habits, really such a contemptible and repressed character, or were ordinary people worth defending precisely in their ordinariness? Was classically liberal, democratic government just one way of ordering political affairs, or was it *the best* way? These were the ideas, challenges, and provocations unfolding in the little magazines every month.

I wanted to join this club, and by a couple years into college, I had my application in order. I'd written a review of the novel *O My America!* by Johanna Kaplan for the *American Spectator,* then famous for its role as a smart-ass but generally highbrow proving ground for young talent. I got eighty dollars for it, which made me a professional writer. And John and I had started on campus a little magazine of our own, which would turn out to be the first of a wave of alternative campus publications Irving Kristol would arrange funding for through the Institute for Educational Affairs in New York. The original name was *Midway,* which captured the flavor of something that was distinctly antileft but was also not conservative in the Young Republicans sense. The school, in a fit of fussiness, made us give up that name on account of a University of Chicago Press imprint called Midway Books. We rechristened it *Counterpoint,* which likewise captured the spirit of the enterprise fairly well: something different from the left-wing opinion preponderant on campus.

We chose as the magazine's epigraph/motto a quotation from George Orwell. John, of course, had more than once read through the four volumes of Orwell's collected essays, journalism, and letters before he even got to Chicago, and from one of the well-thumbed paperbacks we extracted this: "The essential fact to which we have got to cling, as to a life-belt, is that it is possible to be a normal decent person and yet to be fully alive." To me, the passage is as alive today as it was a quarter century ago when we picked it.

Allan Bloom arrived at the Committee on Social Thought my second year at Chicago. His reputation preceded him: John's mother, Midge Decter, was his editor at Basic Books when he was producing his translation of Plato's *Republic.* I had pretty much wasted my first year academically, taking pretentiously attractive-sounding classes such as "Conceptual Foundations of the Social Sciences," where we studied (among other things) the *Umwelt* of the spiderling. It's what happens when you leave a young person to fend for himself without sensible guidance. At least the class was easy.

No thanks to the college and much to Midge Decter, my guidance had improved sufficiently by my second year to understand I should check out Bloom. There were maybe a dozen of us in the class, which was to entail a close reading of Plato's short dialogues *Ion, Euthyphro,* and *Laches.* I wasn't sure I was following Plato very well, but Bloom—what an impossibly brilliant, hilarious, scandalous, and magnetic character.

I more or less majored in Bloom during the rest of my undergraduate days. Formally, my field of concentration (Chicagoese for "major") was political science—a department that had tried without success to block Bloom's appointment and that cross-listed his Committee on Social Thought offerings in political philosophy only grudgingly. It didn't matter: There was Bloom on Nietzsche, Bloom on Thucydides, Bloom on Machiavelli, Bloom on Rousseau, a feast of detailed scrutiny of passages from the volume in question—generally one book per quarter, no more, and you can understand the added appeal there—interlaced with a devastatingly witty elitist critique of modernity, the university, and modern manners. "Most people are so proud of quitting smoking," Bloom said between cigarettes, "because it's the only thing they have ever *achieved* in their lives." He would eventually write up this critique and publish it as *The Closing of the American Mind,* that least plausible of number-one best sellers.

I should say that I wasn't an especially good student of Bloom's. He was a famously demanding grader, and I never mustered better than a B-plus/A-minus (Bloom knew how to split hairs). He delivered his judgment accompanied by a withering though mercifully brief set of comments indicating the gross insufficiency of one's understanding of the material.

To be sure, Bloom, in a trope of his hermeneutical school, claimed that he understood no more than a quarter of Machiavelli himself. Bloom could not help being extravagant even in humility. The effect of this claim on his students—well, at least on me—was anything but heartening, because if the great Bloom understood a mere fourth of Machiavelli, would the percentage comprehension of his students (meaning me, again) ever even crack double digits?

Bloom often railed against my facility as a writer. I wrote too quickly, too easily, I needed to slow down. (This was, by the way, long before I actually learned to write quickly, a by-product of the responsibility of getting an editorial page and an op-ed page to press every night.) If one wrote too quickly, so too did one read too quickly, too superficially. Again, one must slow down, read every word, think about every line—for when the great philosophers wrote, they did not do so casually, but rather to conduct a great dialogue with each other across the ages, a dialogue in which few were privileged to participate in even the slightest degree, let alone at the highest level.

To know of the existence of this great dialogue, to have been persuaded that participation in it was the highest activity of the mind imaginable, and yet to feel oneself inadequate to participate in it—this was quite painful at the time. I had found something that was simultaneously compelling, in that I couldn't get enough of it, and beyond my reach, in that it was never, ever easy, and I never felt like I was any good at it. The experience was emotionally draining, a kind of protracted exercise in the cultivation of humility in someone for whom, in truth, the sensibility had been alien. Oh, I knew something about the way in which the world could inflict pain capriciously, all right, and according to my neo-Calvinist view of human nature at the time, people could mainly be depended upon to disappoint you in one way or another. This was dark. But there was a redemptive element somewhere—within. I thought I could handle it, whatever "it" was. Thanks to Bloom, I lost that sense of self-assurance.

This was, on balance, a very good thing. The reason is that I had a chance to rebuild it in myself. In the first instance, it was more or less mine as a given, and that's too easy. You probably know people who were born with the intellectual equivalent of a silver spoon in their mouth and never had occasion or took occasion to wonder why it was there. The quality, which goes by the name of intellectual arrogance, is not attractive. Once my spoon was gone, however, I had a real choice: acquiescing in the ensuing uncertainty or trying to reacquire a sense of self-assurance by dint of work. I chose the latter.

Bloom thought I should go on to pursue a Ph.D. in political philosophy at the University of Toronto. Two other prominent members of his school held forth there. I began the process of application without real enthusiasm. And I gave it up happily when Irving Kristol offered me a job as assistant editor of *The Public Interest* in New York, my very own slot on the bottom rung of the ladder of New York intellectual life and official status as a card-carrying neoconservative. No, it was not the *vita contemplitiva*. On the other hand, I have learned quite as much about politics from the close observation of and, at some level, participation in contemporary affairs as from the study of old books—or rather, the study of old books alone would likely yield insight as partial as that which one might achieve by action alone, without reference to old books at all.

Bloom was disappointed when I told him I was going to New York. Perhaps he didn't think I was as bad a student as I thought he thought. It was our last conversation. I don't think it's just by virtue of hindsight that I can say that going to New York to match myself against the town (something every young writer feels impelled to do, as Saul Bellow once said in an interview with a certain *Midway* magazine) was my first real step of intellectual independence. To have gone to Toronto would have entailed a passive acquiescence, submission to some other view of me than my own. No thanks.

⟫⟶

As it happened, by the time I turned forty-one, I felt much better. I was well on the way toward resolving the first serious crisis of my professional career, which arose only after my fortieth birthday. In retrospect, it was the resolution of that crisis that closed the gap between *becoming* and *being*.

The crisis and resolution were the transfer of the journal I had taken over and revamped in 1999, *Policy Review*, from its institution of origin, the Heritage Foundation, which no longer wished to publish it, to its new home at Stanford University's Hoover Institution and my appointment as a fellow there in April 2001. Suffice it to say that there is nothing I would rather be doing than editing *Policy Review* as a Hoover Institution publication, nor any affiliation I would prefer. If this sounds like the language of someone who is happy with the choices he has made and the doors he has closed behind him, that's correct.

To achieve such results, you must take responsibility for your happiness. There are no guarantees of success, of course. But there's a certain pleasure in the act of taking responsibility all on its own. It's the pleasure of freedom.

The Most Dangerous Psychiatrist in America

SALLY SATEL

Sally Satel, M.D., is a practicing psychiatrist and the W. H. Brady Fellow at the American Enterprise Institute. She is author of *PC, M.D: How Political Correctness Is Corrupting Medicine,* and coauthor with Christina Hoff Sommers of *One Nation Under Therapy: How the Helping Culture Is Eroding Self-Reliance* (St. Martin's, 2005).

LET ME INTRODUCE myself. I am the most dangerous psychiatrist in America. At least that's what a former director of the federal Center for Mental Health Services, a psychiatrist himself, called me in 1999. Alas, I considered him one of the most mediocre psychiatrists in America, so the label lost some of its delicious sting.

Four years later, I was the subject of a protest outside the Moscone Convention Center in San Francisco, the site of an annual meeting of the American Psychiatric Association. The aggrieved were former psychiatric patients who decried certain mental health policies I had advanced in a recent book (about which more later).

One protester was supposed to be me. He had taken my headshot off the internet, enlarged it, and was now wearing it as an oversized Sally Satel mask. Posing for photos in an ill-fitting dress with a big lapel badge that said "Right Wing Lunatic," he was handing out mock Prozac capsules the size of cocktail franks.

Me? In an ill-fitting dress! That's bad enough. But "right wing"?

Now, the charge of "dangerous psychiatrist" was one I could embrace, as I will explain. Still, I hadn't ever been called right wing before. Yes, the descriptor "conservative psychiatrist" did pop up occasionally, but that was off the mark as well.

More properly, I am a *contrarian* psychiatrist. And in this essay I will explain how I became one.

>>→

Politically speaking, I was a very late bloomer. My parents were Jewish New York Democrats—as was everyone I knew during my Queens childhood. No one in my family was especially passionate about politics and I can hardly remember it being the subject of discussion at dinner or at family gatherings. What I do remember, though, was being repelled by the anti-Americanism of the Vietnam War protests. My father was very patriotic and law-abiding; a child of the Depression, he could never seem to get over the abundance of everything in this country: cars, clothes, food, and, mostly, opportunity. We had fun mocking the sixties hippie culture and its tie-died aesthetic, which had blossomed by the time I was in sixth grade. To this day, the smell of pot smoke reminds me of lazy, glassy-eyed flower children.

I went to high school in the early seventies. Thankfully, the social stratification was not as rigid as that portrayed in Hollywood teen movies. Still, it would be fair to say that if I were cast in a film with Lindsay Lohan, I'd be at the lunch table reserved for the unclassifiables: neither nerd nor cool. I was too studious to be cool. My parents hadn't gone to college but there was no doubt I would.

In retrospect, my father—a commercial graphic artist by day but on weekends a great indoorsman with a lust for *National Geographic* magazines (there were five-feet-high columns of yellow in his closet; he saved every issue of the magazine since 1941 with its telltale yellow binder facing out)—was grooming me to be the next Jane Goodall. He often took me to the American Museum of Natural History, the Bronx Zoo, and the Coney Island aquarium. Every Sunday night we watched Mutual of Omaha's *Wild Kingdom*. On the first Earth Day in April 1970, we went to Union Square to hear Mayor Lindsay and Paul Newman address the rally.

Three years later I was off to the Agricultural College at Cornell in upstate New York, thinking that I would be an animal behaviorist. The Ag School, unlike the College of

Arts and Sciences, was no hotbed of political activism, and the poisonous racial tensions on the Cornell campus had eased before I got there.

It took only one course in animal behavior (wherein our first assignment was to collect wolf spiders hiding in the grass by shining a flashlight in their eyes—all eight of them!) before I, the consummate arachnophobe, quit. Despite my father's noble efforts, I remained a sheltered, city naturalist. Moreover, I was in shameless sympathy with satirist Fran Lebowitz's definition of the "outdoors": the space between the cab and the hotel. In 1977 I graduated with a B.S. in biology and went to the University of Chicago to study evolutionary biology from the safety of a lab.

But I didn't love it enough—a prerequisite for graduate work—and soon I was intrigued by the experiences of friends who instead attended the university's medical school. The practical nature of their work was appealing. Even though I liked the romance of being a scientist, the worldly importance of my day-to-day work dissecting the oral musculature of tadpoles—which, trust me, had potential relevance to understanding how organisms evolve under various environmental conditions—was too hard to explain to inquiring relatives, and, increasingly, myself. And when one med student told me in great depth about a patient he was evaluating for major depression during his psychiatry clerkship, I saw that psychiatry was a field with enormous scope—to practice it well one had to possess an intoxicating range of knowledge from neurobiology to brain anatomy to physiology to pharmacology to diagnostic schemes to Shakespearean tragedy. Soon after, I applied to medical school and in 1984 I graduated from Brown as a doctor. In 1988, I completed my residency at Yale and soon became a board-certified psychiatrist.

$$\gg\rightarrow$$

I didn't meet a Republican until 1992, when I was thirty-six. By that time I had been an assistant professor of psychiatry at Yale for five years, assigned to a clinical position at the veterans' affairs medical center, one of the Yale teaching affiliates.

I vividly remember meeting My First Republican. His name was Herbert Kleber, a senior professor of psychiatry at Yale. We were walking up Broadway in San Francisco during the second week in May while in town for the annual meeting of the American Psychiatric Association (this was years before the protest outside the convention center when, coincidentally, the meeting was also in San Francisco). Our conversation turned to Herb's former position in the drug czar's office in the first Bush administration. "Does this mean you are a Republican?" I asked him, wide-eyed. We were right across the street from City Lights bookstore when Herb whipped it out. The voter registration card said: Republican.

Psychologists call this a "flashbulb memory," a memory laid down in sharp detail during an event of great personal significance. (A standard question meant to elicit a shared flashbulb memory in people born in the fifties or before is, "Where were you when President Kennedy was shot?") Meeting my first Republican was so momentous, it had the quality of a presidential flashbulb memory. But apart from the surprise of encountering a species I had previously observed only on *Crossfire* and *Meet the Press,* I saw that the Republican could be thoughtful and funny ("we'll double-cross that bridge when we come to it," was one of Herb's favorite quips), not to mention well respected in our field, even if he was a political noncomformist.

The early nineties was the period of what one might call my political awakening.

First, I started to feel limited in my job in academic psychiatry. I had spent four wonderful years as a resident in psychiatry at Yale and five years as an assistant professor working out at the West Haven Veterans Administration Medical Center. My first research projects on cocaine addiction involved describing the features of cocaine-induced paranoia. They were fun and novel, but when a new boss took over he had other ideas about what was interesting and wanted me to investigate pharmaceutical treatments for addiction. In rote, assembly-line fashion we tried one medication after the next to see if it suppressed craving for cocaine; nothing worked, and almost two decades later, there's not been much progress.

Another depressing feature of my faculty work at West Haven was the entitlement culture endemic to the veterans' affairs system. As a colleague once wrote in the now-defunct *Public Interest,* "At the VA it Pays to be Sick" (Douglas Mossman, Winter 1995). He was referring to the infamous service-connection benefits available to veterans who were (partly or fully) incapacitated during their military service. No one, of course, begrudges injured veterans treatment and financial support if they cannot work. But the seduction of "total and permanent disability" benefits (which come to about thirty thousand dollars a year, tax-free, plus health care) was irresistible, and a lot of patients who probably could have been rehabilitated found themselves living, instead, as subsidized psychiatric invalids.

Then in the fall of 1992, a homeless Vietnam-era veteran named Larry Hogue was in the news. A relatively docile panhandler when not smoking crack, Hogue became aggressive and psychotic when he was on the pipe. He terrorized the Upper West Side of Manhattan, screaming obscenities, setting fires beneath cars, and masturbating in front of children. Once he pushed a girl into traffic. The police took Hogue to jail or to the hospital dozens of times, but he was always released two days later to live and sleep and urinate on the streets. Dubbed "The Wild Man of Ninety-sixth Street" by the tabloids, Hogue reportedly received three thousand dollars a month from his veteran's pension. His crack dealer got most of it.

At that time, I was working in West Haven as director of an inpatient psychiatric ward designated for the treatment of drug addiction and alcoholism. Many of my patients were just like Larry Hogue—people who became psychotic and combative when they used alcohol or stimulants. And, like Hogue, once they were sober they became lucid and calm—and the hospital could not keep them against their will. It was theoretically possible to have these "revolving door" patients legally committed against their will under a so-called grave disability standard—that is, an established pattern of becoming a threat to one's self or others—but the civil liberties lobby fought this mechanism tooth and claw, protecting the patients' fragile "autonomy." As a result, enforcement of such civil laws had become notoriously weak.

The Larry Hogue story was covered in the *New York Times* and on CBS's *Sixty Minutes.* It was clear that the controversies sparked by his case went beyond mental health care: They reflected a certain set of social values and political ideas—a part of the "culture war," as it was starting to be known. Underlying these debates were differing notions of human freedom and citizenship, personal responsibility and agency, and the proper role of institutions in supervising those who cannot govern themselves. Many of my fellow psychiatrists either were silent or sided with civil libertarians, but a vocal minority pressed for overhaul of such policies. I wanted to join in that debate. When I published an op-ed piece about Hogue in the *Wall Street Journal*—arguing that, by law, he should be required to undergo long-term treatment and supervision by the mental health system—I was excited to be a small part of it. It was my first heady taste of public dialogue.

There was one more formative event that had nothing whatever to do with me personally: the 1993 water buffalo case at the University of Pennsylvania. At the center of the incident was a hardworking freshman who was disturbed at night by rowdy African-American students outside his dorm room. He yelled at them to "shut up, you water buffalo"— the student was Jewish and "water buffalo" was likely a loose translation of the word "fool" or "cow" in Hebrew or Yiddish. But many interpreted this unusual phrase as a racist slur of some sort. A politically correct conflagration ensued replete with toxic race politics, a show trial for the offending freshman, and enforcement of an Orwellian speech code that prohibited any behavior "that has the purpose or effect of . . . creat[ing] an intimidating . . . environment," according to university regulations.

I read that one could contribute to the Penn student's legal defense fund through a group called the National Association of Scholars, a contrarian academic organization founded in 1987 by political scientist Stephen Balch to counter exactly this sort of excess of political correctness. I joined the NAS and discovered an impressive group of academics fighting politicization of scholarship and teaching on campus. In contrast to my education at Cornell, imparted by first-rate biology and English professors who kept their politics to themselves, I learned that many campuses were corrupted by faculty members and administrators who were contemptuous of intellectual diversity among their colleagues and students.

My medical career, too, was largely protected from the miasma of political correctness. In hospitals and clinics, there wasn't much room for postmodernism or hand-wringing over race-class-and-gender. We had concrete tasks to do and these had measurable, often life or death, outcomes. Still, the embattled college faculty and students needed to mount a defense against threats to academic excellence, campus civility, and free inquiry, and I wanted to be a part of that effort.

A culture warrior was born.

⋙→

I do not consider myself an activist, however. If anything, I am a *re*activist. Had I not been dismayed by deterioration of clinical judgment in my field and by policies creating so many unintended consequences, I doubt I would have ever left the confines of research and patient care.

I didn't so much turn right in the nineties as assume a political identity that reflected my ideals of personal freedom and responsibility. As a psychiatrist for people who are severely mentally ill or addicted, and as a psychotherapist for the worried well, my goal was to broaden my patients' capacity for self-determination—and their acceptance of responsibility for those choices. A key part of the psychiatrist's role is to perceive how persistent illness can place limits on the capacity for freedom. Then the work is to help the patient maximize his autonomy within those bounds.

All my writing is done as a physician. My medical training and experience are what give me authority to comment on public health issues. And nearly everything I have written is a reaction—sometimes a rebuke—to those in my profession who are either poorly informed, at best, or, at worst, allow their political agendas to blind them to patients' best interests and to accurate representation of the latest science.

This public defiance of what I believe to be failures of medical excellence and academic professionalism has gotten me labeled a "conservative psychiatrist." But it is an illusion. I arrive at my positions because they make sense, not because they confirm a pre-existing political outlook. I only appear conservative because mainstream mental and public health entities are so closely allied with traditional liberal pieties. Surveys of psychologists reveal that the vast majority consider themselves "liberal." Calling me conservative is nothing more than a way to estrange my ideas by naming them the product of what many of my colleagues believe to be a malign political orientation.

Recall how psychiatrists were the ones who attacked Republican presidential candidate Barry Goldwater. In 1964, one month before the election, the now-defunct magazine *FACT* published a survey of members of the American Psychiatric Association and what they thought of Goldwater's mental fitness for the presidency. The article was called "The Unconscience of a Conservative," a play on the title of Goldwater's 1960 autobiography *The Conscience of a Conservative.* The psychiatrists savaged Goldwater, calling him "warped," and a "paranoid schizophrenic" who harbored unconscious hatred of his Jewish father and had endured rigid toilet training. Interestingly, the late senator Goldwater, much beloved by all his colleagues, has been resurrected in mainstream analyses in recent years because of his pro-choice libertarianism—one wonders if psychiatrists would consider him warped now.

≫→

I was closely involved with the National Association of Scholars from about 1995 to 1998. Its president, Steve Balch, asked me to write about the intrusion of political correctness into the medical arena. As an example, he mentioned the alternative medicine movement as emblematic of hostility to Western science and rationalism. I attended a conference on alternative medicine and wrote about its driving animus—a rejection of American medicine as a symbol of the "medical heteropatriarchy." It was a fun—if maddening—project, but I remember telling Balch that I wasn't quite sure I could think of other examples of PC medicine.

Then I encountered the San Francisco General Hospital. Psychiatrists in charge of the psychiatric wards were grouping inpatients according to race and sexual orientation. It was 1995, though hospital-based segregation by race had ended in the 1960s. Patients were assigned to treatment units (or "teams") specializing in their specific group identity—blacks, Asians, Latinos, gays/lesbians/bisexuals, women, and the HIV-positive. (Straight, white, HIV-negative males, the only patients without a "team" of their own, were assigned to other teams on the basis of bed availability.) Each team was guided by a "curriculum" that specified the proper procedures for treating members of the relevant group. Efforts were made to match staff and doctors by their own sex, race, and sexual preference to the appropriate group.

The curriculum for the Black Focus Unit, as it described itself, was designed to "address the issue of racism as it affects mental health professionals emotionally. . . . The resulting enhanced personal awareness of racism will improve the therapeutic alliance with the African-American mental health client." One of the unit's "educational objectives" for the staff was to "break down denial of one's own participation in racism." A colleague who works at San Francisco General tells me these units are still operating today. Unbelievable.

Soon, I became aware of scores of other manifestations of victim politics in medicine. There were women's health advocates who contended, incorrectly, that the male-dominated medical establishment has kept women from participating as subjects in research studies, thus depriving them of the benefits of medical breakthroughs. There were nurses who claimed they were oppressed by the hierarchical nature of that medical establishment and rebelled by mocking "heteropatriarchal ways of knowing" and practicing New Age, scientifically fraudulent techniques on nonconsenting patients. I discovered public health professors forthrightly teaching their students that income redistribution is the key to improving population health and promoting the study of unscientific concepts such as the effect of "powerlessness," "classism," and "racism" on health.

Though these "indoctrinologists," as I came to call them, passionately believed they were fighting for better health through social justice, their actions had little practical relation to preventing disease, treating symptoms, or improving clinical research. At best they created distractions and wasted money; at worst they interfered with effective care and justified patients' passivity by absolving them of any responsibility for their health. In either case, the indoctrinologists undermined the Hippocratic ideal, which puts the patient first. Soon I had a book's worth of material and I wrote *PC, M.D.—How Political Correctness Is Corrupting Medicine* (Basic Books, 2001).

The book took a panoramic view of medicine. But I could have written a small volume on mental health alone and devoted a chapter or two to the American Psychiatric Association, an organization with which I have an ambivalent relationship. Every few years I pay membership dues if I like the president (who is elected for a one-year term). A number of them have been first-rate thinkers and clinicians and many of the members are smart and compassionate professionals. But, as in most health organizations, the leadership is dominated by liberal orthodoxy, and the policy statements that emerge are often diluted by mealy-mouthed consensus and leavened with a generalized fear of offending. Hence, the association has endorsed what I believe to be some very ill-conceived positions. And I am happy to be the media go-to girl for commentary on them.

For example, in 2004 I was asked by reporters to commit on an amicus brief submitted to the Supreme Court by the American Psychiatric Association arguing that the brain of the average seventeen-year-old is too immature to render him fully morally accountable. At issue was whether executing sixteen- and seventeen-year-old murderers violated the Eighth Amendment's proscription against cruel and unusual punishment.

The case involved a teen who burglarized the house of a neighbor. When she awoke, he and a younger accomplice tied her up, drove to a railroad bridge, and pushed her into a river to her death, following a plan they had made before the break-in. The psychiatrists, joined by other medical professionals, detailed description of normal adolescent brain development in their briefs, explaining how the frontal lobes of the teen brain—the region that helps curb impulses, make plans, and weigh risks—are "one of the last parts of the brain to reach maturity."

Using brain imaging to argue a killer is "less guilty by reason of adolescence" struck me as the next evolutionary stage in the abuse-excuse argument. Courts should and do recognize the relevance of brain function in sentencing. Killers who are psychotic or who have a diminished capacity for moral calculus or self-restraint deserve, and generally receive, leniency. In such cases, experts conduct careful neurological, medical, and psychiatric evaluations of those individuals. Similarly, when we suspect significant neurological deficits in a teen who has committed murder, we should consider the circumstances individually, not grant brain-based leniency to an entire class of potential defendants.

The court did rule that executing minors was unconstitutional, but it did not appear swayed by the brain scans. Rather it was moved, five to four, by the fact that a national consensus had developed against the execution of juvenile offenders.

I am eager to expose muddled thinking; does that make me a "conservative psychiatrist"?

≫→

I have always practiced psychiatry, though only on a part-time basis since leaving Yale in 1993. And though a psychiatrist with my sensibilities inevitably runs into critics, the good news is that I enjoy many supporters, too. Not all agree with me, but they do welcome responsible contrarian views. And there are many front-line clinicians out there who appreciate common sense in the name of patient care and clinical research even if they find themselves needing to temper their own views lest they irritate their more ideological chairmen or grant review committees.

Beginning with my West Haven experience, as I have said, I was struck by the power of well-meaning institutions to create conditions that actually made people sicker. These were not problems to be fixed at the level of the individual clinician; they required changes in policy or even legislation. So I applied for a congressional fellowship program run by the Robert Wood Johnson Foundation in 1992. Five years at West Haven was enough.

During my year in Washington, D.C., from 1993 to 1994, I was assigned to the office of Senator Nancy Kassebaum of Kansas. I volunteered to work with her staff because none of the six other RWJ fellowship participants would be caught dead with a Republican. But I, the eager-to-please former pre-med who had actually met a Republican six months earlier, boldly agreed to do it. I had also heard wonderful things about the senator. The RWJ people were grateful for my martyrdom and relieved that they could point to me as the fellow working for a Republican (the year before they had been sued for being too cozy with Ira Magaziner's efforts to develop the Clinton health care plan so they were alert to accusations of continuing partisanship).

It was a tremendous fellowship year. Though designed to introduce university-based health policy experts and physicians to the basics of health policymaking so they could return to their universities and teach it, I knew that I was not going back to New Haven. After nine years I wanted to leave the academic medical setting. My time on the Senate staff was eye-opening, as it is to all outsiders— learning about legislative process, the culture of the Hill and the nature of political power, meeting new people, and learning how research evidence does and doesn't influence decisions.

I was assigned to work on reauthorization of a mental health funding bill. One of the ideas that a staffer and I were trying to build into the bill was the requirement that states develop a plan for implementing enlightened commitment laws. Such laws were intended for people like Larry Hogue—that is, individuals who became reliably psychotic and dangerous when they took illicit drugs or when they stopped their antipsychotic medication. The laws could require them to take medication or be supervised, but the key innovation was that the patients would still be able to live in the community rather than an institution.

What impressed me was the vast contrast between the Republican staff and the Democrat staff (especially Senator Kennedy's people, our main counterparts on the Labor and Human Resources Committee and the mental health "advocates" who were allied with him). Defying the stereotype of liberals that I had brought with me to Washington, the Democratic staffers who worked on mental health were anything but soft and touchy-feely. They seemed perpetually angry. They were often dismissive and arrogant toward me and the staff from Republican offices and unaware how little they knew about the real world of mental illness. And they bristled at the very idea of coercion for patients who posed a severe threat to themselves. The conservative staff, to my amazement, viewed the severely mentally ill with far more compassion (this may have been less a reflection of their political worldview than the fact that many were practicing Christians). They were respectful of my expertise in psychiatry and of colleagues I consulted to help shape the amendment.

My Hill experience gave me a startling insight: Liberals and conservatives seemed to have mirror-image approaches to paternalism. Liberals made intrusive laws for the competent while conservatives preferred to rely on individuals to make their own decisions. Conversely, conservatives preferred intrusive laws for the incompetent to whom liberals applied a hands-off policy. Liberals were comfortable with public health paternalism: intrusive nonsmoking laws, taxes on unhealthy products, strict risk-averse EPA and FDA regulations. Their counterpart practitioners in the clinic were quick to sign forms for disability (without insisting on a trial of vocational training first), pathologizing everyday upsets, and in a million little ways infantilizing patients and focusing on their past, their childhood traumas, and their vulnerabilities rather than concentrating on their future and their strengths.

Yet, when a person was incoherent, defecating in the streets, or freezing a limb off in the park, then—and only then—did the principles of autonomy apply. Well, at least they "died with their rights on," said a colleague, mocking the ACLU. I was shocked by the arrogance of policymakers

and disability advocates who were willing to sacrifice patient dignity and civic order for their idea of personal freedom. (Years later I saw the limits of right-wing ideology
when some conservative politicians attacked drug companies and clinicians for their use of medications like Ritalin
and Prozac to treat children, claiming that there is no legitimate use of these drugs for children. Clearly, there is.)

≫→

After completing my Hill fellowship in December 1994, I
wasn't quite ready to leave the academic world. I got a job
as a visiting faculty member in the Department of Psychiatry at the University of Pennsylvania (Philadelphia being
a symbolic geographic compromise between Washington
and New Haven). A few months at Penn were all I needed to
resolve my ambivalence: I wanted to be in Washington. I
moved back in the summer of 1995 and had a series of envi-
able jobs, each one serendipitously coming along as the previous one was ending. In 1995–96 I was the staff psychiatrist
at the District of Columbia drug court, one of the earliest
offender-diversion programs of its kind. In that year of the
Republican sweep, I was asked to testify before Congress
several times on the subjects of drug-addicted mothers in
the context of welfare reform and on the SSI program. In
1996, I also worked for the Senate Veterans Affairs Commit-

tee, chaired by the irreplaceable Senator Alan Simpson; in 1997–99 I was given a stipend to write *PC, M.D.* at the Ethics and Public Policy Center, which was then run by Elliott Abrams, who made my stay there an author's dream.

I have been in my current position at the American Enterprise Institute since 2000. I am indebted to Christopher DeMuth, whose wise leadership of AEI allows me and my colleagues—some of the most accomplished policy experts in Washington—complete intellectual freedom.

So what am I? Formally, I am a Republican. I switched parties soon after my fellowship with Senator Kassebaum. Honestly, though, I could have just as easily become a conservative Democrat or an Independent. If there were a Humane Utilitarian party, I would join it.

I agree with sociologist James Davison Hunter that the worldviews of liberals and conservatives stem from different values. As he put it in his perceptive book, *Culture Wars: The Struggle to Define America,* the political poles reflect "two different ways of apprehending reality, of ordering experience, of making moral judgments." To visualize this, imagine a series of continua with liberals on one end and conservatives on the other. Consider, for example, ideas about the formation of human character. Liberals fall on the side of the continuum that emphasizes the influence of environment in its formation. On the other side are conservatives, who emphasize the primacy of innate traits and free will. Or take principles of relating to others. On one side of this axis is nurture (liberals); on the other, discipline (conservatives).

Then there is the axis labeled the proper role of government; liberals tout the government's caretaking responsibilities (and the regulation and social entitlements that come with it), while conservatives most value its duty to protect and extol self-reliance and market competition. Liberals value equality of outcomes, or "cosmic justice," as Thomas Sowell calls it, while conservatives value equality of opportunity. Liberals promote the rights of groups while conservatives value autonomy of the individual. In short, today's conservatives are the classical liberals of the eighteenth and nineteenth centuries.

Yet I am an ambivalent member of the Republican Party. I am embarrassed to be in the same camp as moral conservatives and the religious right when I see their role in suppressing federal funding for stem cell research, and their repudiation of assisted suicide and the use of marijuana for legitimate medical purposes. I find their advancement of the concept of intelligent design intolerable. I am pro-choice, pro-Darwin, and pro–stem cell.

Since 1997, I have worked part-time at a local methadone clinic. I am pretty sure that most of the staff would call themselves liberal, but we never discuss politics; we discuss patients. And we almost always agree in our clinical judgment. I suspect this is true because most of the staff were once heroin addicts themselves and recognize the virtues of setting expectations of progress for patients, limits on their behavior, accountability for bad choices, and rewards for self-betterment. In the minds of many mental health and disability advocates, I continue to be the "most dangerous psychiatrist in America," as I read occasionally on specialty Listservs. And I sometimes see myself identified in news stories as "conservative psychiatrist Sally Satel." But at the clinic, I am just "Doctor Satel," "Doc," or "Dr. Sally." And, of course, that is all I ever was.

The Longer Way

PETER BERKOWITZ

Peter Berkowitz teaches at George Mason University School of Law and is the Tad and Dianne Taube Senior Fellow at the Hoover Institution, Stanford University. He is the author of *Virtue and the Making of Modern Liberalism* and *Nietzsche: The Ethics of an Immoralist*. He is the editor of five volumes on American politics, and serves, with Tod Lindberg, as general editor of *Hoover Studies in Politics, Economics, and Society*. His articles, essays, and reviews appear in a variety of publications.

OVER THE YEARS and in a variety of publications, I have taken issue with any number of positions, and purveyors of positions, that would currently be described as "liberal." This engagement has stirred up a fair amount of indignation and enmity on the left. But because I have typically criticized liberals and liberalism for betraying *liberal* principles, the satisfaction generated among those on the right has often been tempered by a certain suspicion. Indeed, shortly after I began to teach political philosophy at Harvard, I had lunch with an established conservative scholar from another university who, after taking my measure, put down his chopsticks, leaned across the table, and put it to me, mostly playfully, "You know what your problem is? You don't hate liberalism enough." Actually, I replied, I don't hate liberalism at all. The more I've thought about politics, the more I've come to believe that conserving liberalism it-self is among our most pressing public tasks.

Of course, the liberalism to which I refer is not what everybody understands by the term. In the United States, a liberal is a man or woman of the left, a progressive, who wants government to take an aggressive role in combating market imperfections and social inequities by ensuring for all citizens a robust level of material and moral well-being. In Europe, the liberal label signifies a rival partisan point of view. On the other side of the Atlantic, a liberal is a kind of conservative, a libertarian and free marketeer, who wishes to firmly limit government regulation of the economy and morals in order to emancipate individual creativity and drive. In the larger and primary sense in which I use the word *liberal,* both American liberals and European liberals count. So today do most American conservatives.

This larger liberalism refers not to a political party but to a centuries-old tradition of political thought and order. The liberal tradition is defined above all by the moral prem-ise that founds it, which is that human beings are by nature free and equal, and the political premise that directs it, which is that the purpose of government is to secure the in-dividual freedom shared equally by all. It is also distinguished by the quarrels over priorities and policies to which it natu-rally gives rise, the qualities of mind and character that it particularly prizes, and the weaknesses and unwise tenden-cies that it typically encourages. This tradition arose in rebellion against the ancient and medieval idea that the aim of politics was to perfect men's nature or save their souls. It developed a new science of politics that grounds sovereignty in the people, that limits government in the name of individual rights, and that protects those rights by, among other means, a variety of institutional mechanisms for separating and blending political power. Its most famous founding father is of course John Locke, and Montesquieu, Madison, Kant, Burke, Tocqueville, and Mill, among others, refined its principles and elaborated its moral and political implications. In the United States, statesmen such as Lincoln, Theodore Roosevelt, Woodrow Wilson, Franklin Roosevelt, Harry Truman, and Ronald Reagan all crafted policies in its defense, though not always invoking it by name.

My own formal introduction to this tradition began, as it did for many others, in college. I arrived at Swarthmore in the late 1970s, Chicago born but suburban bred, a middle-class kid, comfortable though not affluent, a good enough but lazy student, largely reconciled to never playing tennis at world-class levels, more or less indifferent to party politics, and hungry for what exactly I did not know. While dabbling in economics, psychology, and philosophy before settling on English literature as a major, I encountered a small, remarkable band of professors. Influenced by Marx in their formative years but increasingly dissatisfied with Marxist prescriptions, these teachers were united by the conviction that a large set of ideas and political arrangements they called liberalism dominated our lives—and were destructive of our humanity. If you had asked me then, I would have told you that these teachers were men of the left, not because they brought politics into the classroom (which they didn't) but because it would not then have occurred to me, and nothing available on campus suggested, that there was any other vantage point from which to criticize politics, culture, and morals. My teachers conducted their classes in political science and philosophy as if their lives, and the lives of their students, depended on them. Even in their more extravagant criticism of the liberal tradition, they taught us to respect the force of argument, the discipline of learning, and the long, hard road that leads to thinking for oneself. Thus, despite their ostensible repudiation of all things liberal, they provided an enduring image of liberal educators in action.

These teachers had their favorite authors. At the top of the list were Roberto Unger, Alasdair MacIntyre, and Charles Taylor. However much I now differ with them, their work continues to inform my understanding of the system of ideas and sentiments in which we live. The book that had the largest impact on me then was Unger's *Knowledge and Politics.* Unger's remarkable aim was to carry out a "total criticism" of the liberal tradition, one that uncovered its roots, brought to light its deep structure and its fatal flaws, and sketched an alternative form of thought and society. Unger emphasized the need to reduce the rift between the everyday and the extraordinary that he believed the liberal tradition sustained, and he sought, against what he regarded as the liberal tradition's dogmatic derogation of religious faith, to cultivate an openness to faith's claims. Notwithstanding its massive learning and imposing scholarly apparatus, the book was obviously—though not to my uneducated eyes—the work of a romantic visionary. It was greeted with a deafening silence by the academy when it was first published in 1975, and since has been largely ignored or derided by professors of philosophy, political science, and law. I confess to having been captivated by it, perhaps as only a young student could be who had for the first time glimpsed the exhilarating power of ideas to make sense of experience and to summon to new opportunities and obligations.

Unger was and remains a man of the left. Indeed, in his later writings on law, society, and politics, he elaborated a radical program for political transformation that revealed both an aristocratic disdain for the interests and ambitions of ordinary people and a populist contempt for the need to limit governmental power to protect liberty. But *Knowledge and Politics* operated on a plane above partisan politics. The lessons I took from it were decidedly theoretical, certainly not the sort that one concerned with the nitty-gritty of public policy, or for that matter the leading political issues of the day, could love. Yet the book woke me up, and its central contention got me thinking: Perhaps the liberal tradition, despite purporting to provide a complete and accurate account of human existence, did not exhaust the intricacy of our experience or explain the full range and depth of our aspirations.

Following graduation, I traveled to Israel. Like many others, I was seeking fun and romance, and I landed a job—teaching tennis on a kibbutz—that promised both. I also had ulterior motives, which flowed out of the questions about the liberal tradition that my college studies had posed. I wanted to know more about the operation and ideals of kibbutzim, the most successful Western experiment in communal social life. I wanted to study the Jewish tradition, for religion was one of the chief alternatives eclipsed by the liberal view, and I was a Jew raised in a largely secular household who had reached young adulthood ignorant of what my tradition contained. I wanted to delve into the politics and history of Israel, because of the claim it made to provide—where enlightened Europe had failed so catastrophically in the twentieth century and notwithstanding the acceptance and golden opportunity of contemporary America—a life to Jews as Jews of security and dignity. And I wanted to learn Hebrew, because it was the language both of traditional Judaism and of modern Israel. It would not be the last time that I undertook an adventure only to come to conclusions that diverged dramatically from those I expected to confirm.

Mine was not an orthodox introduction to Israel. The kibbutz where I lived lay on the edge of the Negev, bordering the northeast corner of the Gaza Strip. On a typical day, I would rise at 6:00 A.M. in the shack I shared with two other volunteers (they had left for the fields by 4:30 A.M.). I'd hike a few kilometers on a lightly traveled road, running between desert fields planted with wheat and cotton, to catch a seven-twenty bus on its way from Beer Sheva up to Jerusalem. I'd study Hebrew flash cards and verb tables on the two-hour trip along the coastal plain and into the mountains. Upon arrival at Jerusalem's central bus station—crowded with travelers and vendors, noisy and dirty, exotic and exciting—I would rush to the English-language yeshiva where I would sit in on two hours of classes on Midrash and Talmud and then gobble down a quick, old-fashioned, Eastern European lunch of boiled chicken and rice, whereupon, to the consternation of classmates and teachers, I'd race out. Back on a bus by one, I'd whip out my flash cards and verb tables for the return trip. I'd stroll up to the kibbutz tennis court by four, where until nine I'd offer lessons to kids, teenagers, and adults. To the delight of the kids, the mild irritation of the teenagers, and bemused curiosity of the adults, I'd interrupt the action whenever possible to request a pointer on how to pronounce a new Hebrew word or conjugate a difficult verb.

I sensed that I was living a double life, and that it would be wise to keep it to myself. Eventually, I confirmed as much by casually letting a curious kibbutz friend know how I spent my mornings, and followed up that painful experiment by offhandedly mentioning to an inquisitive rabbi at the yeshiva where it was that I was living. My friend's face and the rabbi's contorted in identical fashion, as if I had nonchalantly disclosed my membership in a gang of child molesters. This face-to-face encounter with the knee-jerk contempt for the religious inculcated by secular kibbutzniks, and the equally knee-jerk contempt for secular kibbutzniks inculcated by the orthodox, certainly provoked a round of doubts in my mind about both parties. But not disgust or despair. To the contrary, I was intrigued and hungry to learn more.

Additional observations in Israel, perhaps well-known to others but important for me to see with my own eyes, followed. The kibbutzim, for example, were slowly but steadily unraveling. Having, in the name of Zionism, drained swamps and made deserts bloom, the founders and their children's generation left the generation to come with middle-class prosperity but too little to do or dream. Moreover, religion revealed a dark side. While I glimpsed in Jerusalem the capacity of traditional Judaism to suffuse ordinary life with rhythm and higher purpose, I could not avoid also seeing among pious Jews, and not least the rabbis who led them, a certain tendency to stifle individuality and hem in independent thinking. And the achievement of liberal democracy in Israel could not be taken for granted. It was threatened from without by enemies pledged to its destruction and from within by bitter class, ethnic, and religious divisions.

All this did not cause me to think less of Israel, but it did focus my mind on the fragility of freedom and the extraordinary achievements of liberal democracy in America. Nor did I grow inclined to disparage the goods—community, religion, or a politics driven by something more than acquisition—of which I had come in search. But my experience abroad did help me appreciate the need to balance these goods with the claims of the individual, of reason, and of bourgeois stability and prosperity.

Concluding that more study was needed, I resolved to return to Israel as a graduate student in philosophy at the Hebrew University of Jerusalem. It was there that I stumbled upon the writings of Leo Strauss. Early in the fall semester I was wandering among the stacks on the fifth floor of the social science library on Mt. Scopus, overlooking the Old City in all of its sun-bleached, late-afternoon splendor, when my eyes caught a title similar to that of a yearlong course I was taking on the critique of religion. Perusing the contents of *Spinoza's Critique of Religion,* I was delighted to discover that it dealt with several of the figures and leading themes on my syllabus. The book would save me, I thought, since I could barely understand the Hebrew in which the seminar was conducted. Then I turned to the first paragraph of the 1965 Preface to the English translation: "This study on Spinoza's *Theologico-political Treatise* was written during the years 1925–28 in Germany. The author was a young Jew born and raised in Germany who found himself in the grips

of the theologico-political predicament." The effect was
electrifying: I'm a young Jew, I thought. I was born and
raised in the United States, and I've traveled to Jerusalem.
And now I have a name for the predicament in the grips of
which I find myself.

I could not put down Strauss's brief intellectual autobiography, which traced the arc of his thought as a young
man struggling to make sense of all the large issues that
gripped me as well—liberal democracy, Zionism, Jewish
faith, and Nietzsche and Heidegger's radical critique of faith
and reason. I was particularly struck by the importance
Strauss attached to Nietzsche. Strauss saw Nietzsche as *the*
philosopher of the age, whose monumental attempt to overthrow Western rationalism and biblical faith must be overcome. Strauss's remarkable contention was that Nietzsche's
critique failed because it never broke free of premises that it
shared with biblical faith and Western rationalism. All in
all, Strauss's Preface offered a masterful intellectual perfor-
mance, in which every sentence thrilled and every observation and argument provided a feast for thought. Before the
academic year had ended, and largely innocent of the controversies that swirled about Strauss in the United States—
and the hatred that mere mention of his name routinely
elicited from political scientists and philosophy professors
in America—I had read all three or four books by Strauss
available in the poorly stocked campus library several times
over.

Strauss's reconciliation of the critique of liberalism
with the defense of liberal democracy left a lasting impression on me. He famously preferred the classical political philosophy of Plato and Aristotle to any modern alternative.
And where other scholars flattered liberal democracy, Strauss
criticized its flaws and called attention to goods—prudence,
honor, virtue, duty, faith—that many liberals and democrats
tended to overlook, suppress, or disparage. Yet Strauss concluded on the basis of classical political philosophy that because liberal democracy protected individual freedom—and
therefore the freedom of those who, while respecting the
law, chose to pursue moral and intellectual excellence or
to obey God's command—it was vastly superior to all existing rivals, indeed the only reasonable alternative in modern circumstances. Particularly in light of the devastating
twentieth-century totalitarian temptations of fascism and
communism, liberal democracy deserved grateful devotion
and energetic defense. At the same time, because he didn't
take the liberal tradition's fundamental premises for granted,
because he looked at the tradition from the outside and at a
distance, Strauss was well situated to identify liberal democracy's weaknesses and unwise tendencies. He did so, though,
as a friend who believed that free individuals could acquire
self-knowledge, and that they had the power to take action
to counteract the follies and pathologies to which free societies were vulnerable.

Strauss's defense of liberal democracy implied that

there were moral and political standards distinct from and superior to those taught by the liberal tradition. At the same time, his scholarship provided an unflinching exploration of liberal democracy's characteristic weak points and vices. These deviations from academic orthodoxy continue to infuriate mainstream American scholars. In contrast to the majority of practicing political theorists, who write as if academic liberalism and democratic theory have superseded everything that the rest of humanity has ever thought and said about morality and politics, Strauss's approach proposes instead a conversation or debate between the rival and ultimately incompatible doctrines out of which the history of political philosophy is composed. In beginning by taking thinkers and schools from different times and places on their own terms, in its skepticism about final and fully adequate answers in morals and politics, and in its toleration of competing opinions and ideas, Strauss's approach has long seemed to me to better exemplify the liberal spirit of inquiry than that of his sneering, seething critics.

But was Strauss right, especially concerning Nietzsche? Was it true that Nietzsche's critique drew strength from the classical and biblical sources it presumed to overcome? And if Nietzsche's critique was dependent on these traditions, did it, contrary to the academically accepted and acceptable interpretations of his thought, provide a surprising source of evidence in support of the continuing vitality of those traditions? My efforts to find my own answers, which persisted through master's studies in philosophy at Hebrew University, doctoral studies in political science and law school at Yale, and continuing studies as an assistant professor in Harvard's Department of Government, culminated in my book, *Nietzsche: The Ethics of an Immoralist.**

I concluded that Nietzsche's philosophical explorations—for all their dazzling light—did not attain their most ambitious goal. His proclamation of the death of God was not a skeptical conclusion of fearless thinking, but rather a dogmatic premise that ultimately impeded philosophical inquiry. His moral judgment that the death of God presented both a catastrophe and a unique opportunity for the human spirit borrowed moral categories from the faith that had supposedly been refuted. His attempt to overthrow Socratic and Enlightenment rationalism because of their systematic falsifications exhibited a Socratic and Enlightenment devotion to reason and truth. And his praise of will, hardness, and immorality presupposed a catalog of more or less traditional and demanding virtues that enabled human beings to create order and master fate in a chaotic and merciless world.

These conclusions set me at odds with a wide array of postmodern scholars who, by the mid-1990s, had achieved controlling authority in much of the humanities and in im-

---

*(Editor's note: This book received the 1995 Thomas J. Wilson Prize of Harvard University Press for best manuscript by a new author.)

portant corners of the social sciences and the legal academy. For them, Nietzsche's thought represented the great liberation from the alleged oppressiveness of the liberal tradition. Although the postmodernists tirelessly congratulated Nietzsche for exposing the arbitrariness of all claims to authority, it was my experience, in a variety of contexts, that they lacked patience for, or the slightest interest in, questions about the authority of their interpretations of Nietzsche or, for that matter, their interpretations of just about anything else.

During the years that I was studying Nietzsche, I was also working my way back from the study of first principles and ultimate questions to a livelier interest in everyday politics. The most obvious manifestation of this shift was the decision to go to law school, which I began days after submitting my dissertation. In part, I took this step because I was disenchanted with the academy. Although I have never ceased to regard the teacher-scholar as a noble ideal, what I saw of socialization into the academy too often provided substance to Nietzsche's characterization of a scholar as a man who thinks the thoughts of another and turns them into dust. At the same time, the grubby side of academic life paradoxically helped me to appreciate the dignity of political and commercial life—without losing sight of their grubby sides, too. And I conceived big plans. I wanted to study constitutional and international law, and I intended to continue to study Arabic, which I had begun to learn in graduate school. It was my grand ambition, as a lawyer, to advance peace in the Middle East by fostering economic cooperation between Israel and the Palestinians.

And once again things did not work out exactly as I planned. I entered law school with every intention of practicing law. And I found there, despite an alarming tendency to collapse the distinction between law and politics, a sense of craft and professionalism that I had missed in my graduate studies. But owing to a surprising constellation of circumstances, while a second year student at Yale Law School I was offered a job teaching political philosophy in Harvard's Department of Government. I leaped at the opportunity.

The offer I received required that I begin promptly. So I agreed to spend the fall semester of my third year in law school teaching political philosophy at Harvard. This was made possible by the best and most dangerous elements of a Yale Law School education. In a meeting in his office during the spring of my second year, the dean casually waived the reasonable law school requirement that students enrolled in courses be in residence in New Haven and attend classes. And why shouldn't he have? On the one hand, he trusted Yale law students to use their freedom well. On the other hand, he supposed—as the faculty and administration drummed into our heads—that we members of the Yale Law School community were above the law, for if we weren't, how would we be able to use it to do the right thing?

I joined the Department of Government as a full-time

faculty member in the fall of 1990 and left in the spring of 1999. Anyone interested in the advanced study of political philosophy could not have hoped for a better opportunity than to teach it to Harvard students, whom I regarded as the university's greatest intellectual resource. Their quick grasp, informed curiosity, and desire to inquire before judging made the classroom an exciting place and frequently an educational one—for the teacher. If a professor did his job well, he could count on provoking observations and questions that forced him to see more deeply and think more clearly. In addition, I was fortunate to have two extraordinary senior colleagues who were breaking new ground in studying the connection between the liberal tradition and character. Instead of attacking the liberal tradition for its deficiencies, they sought from different directions to recover its neglected resources. One was Harvey Mansfield, a conservative and one of the country's most original interpreters of the history of political philosophy; the other, Judith Shklar, was a progressive and one of the last academic political theorists to be formed by a European education in history and literature.

In a Cambridge rife with the atrophy of liberal instincts and the dissipation of the liberal spirit, I was increasingly drawn to the orientation that Mansfield and Shklar represented, despite their rather notable differences in style and sensibility. Of course the vast majority of the faculty were on the left. But liberal? Not if you meant by that a spirit tolerant of dissent, keen on the competition between rival opinions and ideas, and committed to maintaining the moral and material preconditions of a free society.

I recall attending a faculty gathering shortly after I arrived in Cambridge in which Mansfield casually—though with mischievous intent—remarked that it was strange that liberals could not bring themselves to admit that the Cold War was a *war* and that the United States had *won* it. As if to confirm his point, the jaws of Mansfield's colleagues collectively crashed to the ground. And, as if on cue, they cast in his direction a collective dirty look, a mixture of fear and disgust, that I had seen before: in law school when I would ask about the holding of the case or the text of the Constitution as opposed to the desirable policy outcome we were debating; and in graduate school among faculty and students when I mentioned Strauss. But where had I seen it first?

The next time I saw that look in Cambridge, I remembered. During a break in the televised Clarence Thomas Senate Judiciary Committee confirmation hearings, I strolled to my local upscale Harvard Square grocery store and found myself drawn into a gathering of self-proclaimed concerned citizens discussing Anita Hill's allegations. One woman asked if anybody could doubt Thomas's guilt. Nobody could—but me. I said that after listening to Thomas's testimony and learning that twelve women from his office would be appearing before the committee the next day to testify on his behalf, I wasn't sure what to think. From every position around the circle, my concerned fellow citizens targeted me with that all-too-familiar dirty look.

And then I remembered: the kibbutznik, the rabbi, and getting trapped by a gaze that cried out, "A barbarian walks among us!" But that was in the Middle East among doctrinaire socialists and ultraorthodox believers. Cambridge, like New Haven, was supposed to be a bastion of American liberalism.

Thus did journeys abroad and through elite education fortify my conviction that the liberal tradition, especially at our universities, was in need of defense—not least from liberals themselves. Although I was certainly not alone or the first in coming to this conclusion, I first formulated this point of view for myself in the *Yale Law Journal* in an essay called "Liberal Zealotry." In it I suggested that in their intolerance for liberalism's critics—I had in mind thinkers such as Strauss, Unger, MacIntyre, and Taylor, but would certainly include today, among others, Michael Oakeshott and Friedrich Hayek—liberals deprived themselves of a splendid opportunity to gain insight into liberal democracy's shortcomings and craft means for counteracting them. In a number of essays in the nineties, several of which appeared in the *New Republic,* and then in a book, *Virtue and the Making of Modern Liberalism,* I sought to demonstrate how this could be done.

I left Harvard in the spring of 1999 in the midst of controversy over the question of my tenure, which had been approved by the Department of Government in the winter of 1997 and turned down by the university president later that spring. In the fall of 1997, I initiated an internal challenge—on strictly procedural grounds—to the president's decision. In September 2003, after a long, drawn-out battle, I lost in the Supreme Judicial Court of Massachusetts.

Admittedly, challenging Harvard—an institution that at the time had about $20 billion in the bank—on its own turf, with the prospect of a court battle in Boston, where most major law firms did business with Harvard, and where many judges, particularly at the appeals court level and at the level of the state supreme court, maintained ties to Harvard Law School, did not present pretty odds. In nevertheless proceeding, I was not moved by the ideologically grounded opposition to my appointment—which I fully expected. Nor did I contend that I deserved tenure—after all, what relatively young scholar would be so bold as to claim that he had met Harvard's official standard, which is equal to the best in the world? Rather, I saw a principle at stake—that a university had a contractual obligation to honor its own rules and procedures. And I made a judgment that under the unusual circumstances in which I found myself, it would have been dishonorable to fail to stand up for that principle.

My dispute with Harvard did not cause me to throw overboard old principles or leap to new conclusions. I thought before the controversy erupted, and think now, that academic freedom is essential, and that courts have no business substituting their judgment about scholarly excellence for that of university officials. As a result of the controversy, I came to understand that both academic freedom and scholarly excellence are imperiled when universities arrogate to themselves, under the cover of academic freedom and with the acquiescence of the courts, an all but unreviewable authority to determine their legal obligations toward faculty and students. Beyond the controversy, I remain convinced that universities have a crucial role to play in liberal democracies, but to play it well they must rediscover, and rededicate themselves to, the separation of scholarship and politics.

Shortly after moving to D.C., I was told by my former editor at the *New Republic,* half amiably and half ominously, "Now that you're in Washington, you will have to choose between being a liberal Republican and a conservative Democrat." To which I replied that I didn't see why party affiliation was any more relevant in D.C. to getting at the truth about politics than it was in Cambridge, Massachusetts. I did not mean to disparage the role of parties. To the contrary, I had come to believe with Mill that liberal democracies always needed both to conserve their achievements and to make progress in living up to their loftiest promises, and that the best way to accomplish these tasks in a free society was to divide the labor between a party of order and a party of progress. Life in the capital amid the corridors of power has only strengthened the belief.

Since moving to Washington, I have concentrated on understanding the excesses of the party of progress and have regularly defended positions associated with the party of order. In controversies ranging from *Bush* v. *Gore* to the war in Iraq, from the legitimacy and necessity of the security fence in Israel to the quest for women's rights in Kuwait, from the reach and requirements of international law to the constitutionality of the Solomon Amendment, I have found myself coming down on what has come to be considered the conservative side of the question, though not always for the reasons favored by most conservatives. It's not that I regard progress as a small matter. Or that I lack respect for tradition. It's that in America both, in my judgment, depend on conserving liberalism, properly understood.

I Was a Teenage Conservative

RICH LOWRY

Rich Lowry is editor of *National Review,* a political analyst for Fox News, a syndicated columnist, and author of the *New York Times* bestseller *Legacy: Paying the Price for the Clinton Years* (Regnery, 2003).

HOW DID I turn right? It seems an odd question to ask, since I never was anything but right. How did the leopard get his spots? He'd probably say, "Dunno—always been there." That's the way I feel about my political convictions.

Of course, no one really emerges from the womb with views on the most just and efficacious level of taxation—or anything else. Opinions come from somewhere, and mine emerged from the primordial ooze of my political nonconsciousness sometime in high school. Thus, the crucible of my political convictions was a public high school outside Washington, D.C., in Arlington, Virginia. This was not exactly the famous Alcove B at City College where Irving Kristol and other public intellectuals came of age with intense discussions of the ins and outs of Marxism. I'm not sure that many kids at Yorktown High School even knew who Leon Trotsky was. Nor were we roiled by any all-consuming issues like the Popular Front, or the Vietnam War.

We weren't roiled by anything that I can recall. Suburban teenage life circa the mid-1980s constituted the backdrop for my "turn": Clearasil, peer pressure to wear the right kind of jeans (Levi's 501's, if I recall), pioneering MTV VJ Martha Quinn, hair bands, and, of course, smelly gym clothes and underage drinking. I wish it were otherwise. It would have made writing this essay a little less humiliating, but there it is.

Subrational affinity and a few irritable mental gestures—to paraphrase Lionel Trilling's famous put-down of conservatism circa 1950—first drew me to the movement. Over time, my drift right acquired real content. It became a great spur to self-education, and in the ideas of postwar conservatism I would find my vocation. But that took time.

My family wasn't particularly political. My father was an English professor at Trinity College in Washington, D.C., my mother a social worker. It wasn't an overtly political household, but I remember them bitterly complaining about inflation and all manner of other ills during the Carter years. I must have picked up on their Republicanism. I remember sitting at a school desk in elementary school, telling my classmates that Richard Nixon was a better president than John F. Kennedy, to general astonishment. I can't possibly have mustered any substantive arguments to support this assertion. Such is the nature of political discourse among nine-year-olds that their rebuttal, in turn, was to claim that the reason I was pro-Nixon was that I shared his first name. The rest of the conversation must have gone something like, "No, it isn't." "Yes, it is." "No, it isn't," and so on.

I had a dim awareness of public affairs as a child and picked up on causes about which I knew nothing: I supported Jerry Ford over Jimmy Carter in a mock election at school in 1976 (I was eight at the time); liked George H. W. Bush more than Reagan in the 1980 Republican primary fight; and loved repeating the slogan of the Iranian revolutionaries, which sounded something like, "Uni-ah with the shah." Little did I know I was playfully parroting the words of a movement that would take American diplomats hostage and become the world's chief sponsor of Islamic radicalism.

But I didn't know anything. I remained in that state for a long time, and was still in it when I first noticed Ronald Reagan. It was sometime during the 1984 re-election campaign. I was aware of Reagan before then, of course, but just as you can first really notice a girl long after you have met and known her, so it was with Reagan and me. His muscular patriotism, self-confidence, ringing defense of freedom, and good humor drew me to him. I was thrilled hearing "four more years" chants at Reagan rallies broadcast live on CNN before I even fully understood what they meant.

What I knew is that I wanted to be a Reagan supporter—that was one of my subrational affinities. In my mind, the syllogism was: Reagan was a conservative; I'd like to be a conservative; what the heck is a conservative?

I had to find out. I went in search of explanations and defenses of conservatism. My first stop was William F. Buckley's program *Firing Line.* Buckley had hour-long discussions with guests and always trumped any liberal antagonists, on the basis of his wit and intellectual flair if nothing else. Here was another figure, like Reagan, who had a magnetism that was the best advertisement for his ideas. The lesson for political movements is that there is no substitute for leaders with that X-factor, and in the mid-1980s Walter Mondale and Tom Braden just weren't cutting it.

Discovering *Firing Line,* in turn, prompted me to seek out Buckley's magazine *National Review.* I coveted a copy. I remember excitedly walking to the local drugstore and finding only the *New Republic.* I chafed at the injustice of it. It was in my high school library that I finally found copies of *NR,* stuck in those hard plastic binders that libraries used to have. I still remember the covers of the first few issues I saw—one on the death of "liberal internationalism" to mark an anniversary of the Vietnam War; another on the Kissinger Commission report on Central America.

I had no idea what "liberal internationalism" was, and barely knew who Henry Kissinger was. Reading *NR* was like feeling my way through an unfamiliar dark room, always bumping into strange objects. There were so many references I didn't get. Rush Limbaugh tells the story of how he felt inadequate when he first started reading *NR*. He assumed some special initiation was necessary to become a reader. I felt the same way, and became determined to initiate myself.

I made it a discipline to read every issue from cover to cover, no matter how difficult or uninteresting a piece it was. I had no interest in cooking—still don't—but would read the "delectations" column on the off chance it had information that I needed to know, even if I didn't know I needed to know it yet. Slowly, I learned the language of American politics and conservatism, and reading *NR* began to become a pleasure rather than a self-imposed obligation.

I began to experience the joy of an argument that *works,* of the logic and facts lining up so that you hit that perfect slipstream of rationality and reality. I loved the feeling of something just making sense. And once I was armed with such an argument I couldn't wait to subject friends and family to it. I've always been competitive, to a fault. I stopped playing chess with my father when I was a kid, because he routinely beat me, and that was too painful. My competitive relish was such that I was a danger to myself and others on any playing field. Now, in political argument, I was armed and dangerous.

Part of what I enjoyed was having information—on, say, gun control, or the latest arms control agreement—that cut against the grain of conventionality. Arlington, Virginia, was hardly Berkeley, California. But it was dominated by liberal federal workers who traveled on the Metro or in their car pools to government jobs across the river in Washington, D.C. The father of a friend once rebuked me, "How can you support Reagan, when he wants to cut your father's job?" It was a shock for him to learn that, no, my father actually didn't work for the federal government.

I had a streak of cussedness. My friends loved the movie *Star Wars*. I hated it. Everyone worshipped the Washington Redskins, whose games were covered in the Monday *Washington Post* only a little less extensively and breathlessly than the Cuban Missile Crisis. I decided to root for the Houston Oilers. "I've never met a Houston Oilers fan," people would tell me, to my satisfaction. My turn right had a similar aspect.

The teachers in my high school were conventionally liberal. I remember an older woman who taught American history. She was pleasant enough and a student favorite, but she brimmed with smug self-satisfaction. When she told the class once that "the Moral Majority is neither" (the anti–Christian right cliché of that time), I thought that the Moral Majority, whatever that was, couldn't be so bad. She brimmed with disdain for Reagan, considering him an idiot whom no thinking person could support. It was my first encounter with the "liberal elite," and I liked the feeling of opposing it.

There was something mushy in its reasoning, something that seemed resistant to hard logic. There was something pious and sentimental about it, ripe for the puncturing. And something naïve—about people's intentions, and about human nature and our ability to mold it to our liking.

I may have been a teenage conservative, but I wasn't a clean-pressed preppy College Republican type. I hated joiners of all kinds. Nothing irked me more than the student government kids, with their earnestness and polish. The glee club made me recoil in horror. I hung out with unpopular kids who weren't jocks, or artistic, or particularly ambitious in any way. If high school had been an ape colony, we would have been those antisocial unattached males lingering on the fringes, envying the dominant males with their mates.

We were given to mostly harmless acts of mayhem. We skipped class and drank lots of down-market beer and other alcohol. I had a double existence. I would be watching a videotaped episode of *Firing Line* and trying to follow the niceties of a discussion between Bill Buckley and the distinguished British journalist Malcolm Muggeridge, when my friends would pick me up at home for a bout of drinking Pabst Blue-Ribbon behind the local strip mall. I would bring two or three copies of the *American Spectator* to read on the beach during a weekend devoted to the (always ineffectual) chasing of girls on the Ocean City, Maryland, boardwalk.

Looking back, it was an almost ideal confluence of goofing off and proto-training for what would be my calling as a career. To this day, when I smell suntan lotion, it brings back those beach weekends: the intense, free camaraderie that is one of the blessings of that age; the laughter over utter nonsense and the endless teasing and provoking of one another; and the sun-baked, waterlogged, gritty-with-sand pages of some magazine.

I wasn't a go-getter, not outwardly at least. I sat silently in the back of the class. It wasn't until I realized that my grades would matter in getting into a good college that I began—to use the cliché of guidance counselors everywhere—"to apply myself." I got my grades up above the merely mediocre, and in preparing for the SATs, I basically taught myself geometry and all the math I had ignored.

College began to matter to me because very soon after watching Bill Buckley and reading *National Review,* I decided I wanted to be an opinion journalist. Nothing, I thought, could be as blissful as to write and persuade for a living. I remember filling out a career-interest form in high school that asked what we thought we would be doing and where we would be living in ten years' time. I wrote, working for *National Review* and living in New York City.

I took to reading every op-ed in the *Washington Post*

and writing out in longhand a slashing response to one of them every day in a spiral notebook. I was careful to try to engage every argument of the author on its merits, even as I was merciless in my counter-rhetoric. School still didn't fully engage me, but only because it wasn't imparting enough substance. I slipped copies of *National Review* or the *Economist* in between the covers of textbooks and slyly read them during slow moments in class.

Reading had always been important to me. The one area of school where I had always reasonably excelled was English, especially as it became more advanced and focused more on literature and less on grammar and spelling (for which I, oddly enough in an editor, have little natural aptitude). I lived in a book-lined household, thanks to my dad.

When I was twelve years old or so, I read the major Mark Twain novels, old fancy-bound copies that my father's father had gotten in a long-ago giveaway from a newspaper. I associated their musty smell with delight. Often, I still put my nose to a book when I open it to see if it has that grand old aroma. I read typical boy material, too, the stories of baseball heroes and of battles in World War II. I loved the Sherlock Holmes stories and methodically read every one, and then moved on to more serious fare. I went through a Joseph Conrad phase—*Lord Jim, Heart of Darkness, Nostromo.* By the time I had decided I wanted to pursue writing for a career, life had become a futile battle to read everything that mattered. I acquired the habit of reading in all possible stray moments. To this day, I read between sets on the weight machines at the gym, and while brushing my teeth.

If adopting unpopular positions had been one attraction of conservatism for me, a few other instinctual factors drew me to it as well. I hated the idea that things went as planned and turned out in the end, a notion deeply embedded in liberalism. It wasn't until later that I learned the phrase—original to early *National Review* editor Frank Meyer and popularized by Buckley—"don't immanentize the eschaton." This was an admonition to avoid believing that the end-of-time redemption promised by prophetic religion could be achieved on this earth with the right mix of social policies. Socialists and liberals couldn't keep their immanentizing hands off the eschaton.

They were guilty of "straight-line thinking," believing that action A will inevitably lead to intended result B. I recoiled from it. I always felt that lines aren't straight, but tend to be crooked. My older brother, Robert, probably had a lot to do with my attitude. He is handicapped and his outsized presence in our small family—just the two of us and my mom and dad—was always a reminder of tragedy, of the presence of unaccountable and undeserved hardship.

Many people would take the same circumstances and believe in the obligation, and the power, of the state to right injustices. I have always been supportive of programs specifically targeted to those who can't help themselves, but otherwise I drew an opposite conclusion, about the heart-break written into our world and the impossibility of wip-ing it away. Anyone maintaining otherwise was a dreamer, a charlatan, or worse. It made intuitive sense to me that peo-ple with the purest of intentions could end up killing and creating hells on earth in the name of Utopia.

My family also contributed to a complicated relation-ship I had with the established order. I didn't like being told what to do, and I still feel an antiauthority tug every time I have to fill out a form, or stand in a line, or obey any petty rule. Deep down, however, I was thoroughly enamored of the bourgeois family and way of life. It is hard to be a con-servative without filial piety. Every family has its pitfalls, but mine was fundamentally happy, and the attraction of cultural radicalism to me was nil. One New Leftist famously called the upscale New York City suburb of Scarsdale "hell." I wouldn't romanticize Arlington, Virginia, but I never thought it was anything but a perfectly fine place to grow up and for families to raise their children.

I had a natural affinity for the two-parent family, since mine was benign, and I hated divorce. I can't tell you exactly what it was about the kids I knew with divorced families, but you could feel the difference. I noticed it first as far back as elementary school, when it seemed the parents of most of my friends had split in the great divorce epidemic of the 1970s. It cast a pall on their households. It's not that the kids weren't happy at all, or that kids in two-parent house-holds didn't have troubles of their own, but the feeling was palpable. There was a rip in the fabric of their lives.

If I had a libertarian streak, then, I had a paternalistic streak, too: My experience with my brother made me realize that some people had to be taken care of and, basically, told what to do, and my experience with my family made me support policies to nudge people in the direction of bour-geois respectability. So I was inclined to decrease the burden of the state on two-parent families, but increase it on the radically dysfunctional, many of whom were already deeply entangled with the state anyway through their dependence on welfare programs.

These were all the urges and tendencies that initially attracted me to conservatism. But subsequent to this at-traction something important happened: Instead of grow-ing out of conservatism, I grew into it. And I did it through books.

I was led from references in *National Review* to certain books, which led in turn to more books. There were the basics, Barry Goldwater's *The Conscience of a Conservative,* Buckley's *Up from Liberalism,* Russell Kirk's *The Conserva-tive Mind.* But these were just an entrée. James Burnham's accessible polemic *Suicide of the West*—a broad-gauged attack on liberalism, especially its foreign policy—led me to his *The Managerial Elite,* a sophisticated work of sociology, and then on to *The Machiavellians,* a work of philosophy. Before I knew it, I was lounging away summer afternoons on the roof of my parents' back porch trying to follow Burnham's explications of the thought of Robert Michels and Vilfredo Pareto.

What was most gratifying about the intellectual journey associated with my conservatism was the feeling of entering into geocentric orbit with reality. Conservatism accorded with the way the world works (to quote the title of another classic conservative book), so long as you took the time to have a deeper understanding of the world. I remember reading Henry Hazlitt's free-market tour de force *Economics in One Lesson,* and the feeling of lightbulbs going off page by page. Hazlitt wrote that the key to so much of the misunderstanding of economics was "the fallacy of overlooking secondary consequences," and then destroyed the case for tariffs, rent control, "saving" troubled industries, public works projects, and so on, all of which did more economic harm than good once you looked beyond their immediate benefits.

A similar experience was prompted by Charles Murray's *Losing Ground,* a demolition of the liberal welfare state. According to Murray, the best intentions of the crafters of welfare programs had helped trap the poor in broken families and in idleness. This is relatively uncontroversial argument now, but was a revelation in the mid-1980s. Murray's detailed examination of welfare exploded all the soft-minded clichés about it, and lent credence to one of the axioms of the historian Robert Conquest—that the more you know about a subject, the more likely you are to have conservative views on it.

Today, I doubt that former Clinton treasury secretary Robert Rubin would disagree with much in Hazlitt, or that many Democrats would disagree with the bulk of Murray's analysis. Indeed, once you delved into the substance, it was especially easy to become a conservative in the mid-1980s, because they were conservative glory days. Contentious conservative positions from that era have enjoyed a festival of vindication.

A low-tax, less-regulated economy would grow faster. The key to reducing crime wasn't "root causes," but a crackdown on criminals. Gun control had nothing to do with crime. Welfare should be reformed to demand work. A bipartisan consensus had grown up around these positions by the end of the 1990s (with perhaps the exception of gun control, which liberals have shelved for political reasons).

Then, there was the Cold War, the issue that made conservatism most appealing. Let's assume for the sake of argument that conservatives were wrong about everything else and right only about the Cold War. That in itself would have bought conservatism's moral standing. The Cold War was an epochal struggle between good and evil, freedom and repression, and one in which the conservative stance was vindicated: loosely, the Reagan synthesis of high defense spending, aggressive pushback against the Soviets with anticommunist insurgencies, and moral steadfastness, all leavened with prudence and tactical flexibility.

In the 1980s, young conservatives like me were also in a position to pocket liberal successes. Social welfare programs were already taking care of the neediest of the needy. The civil rights revolution had put American society on a more just basis. Environmentalism had cleaned up the air and the rivers. All of that was to the good. A conservative in the 1980s could simply react to liberal excesses in all of these areas: the drive to grow entitlements to include more and more of the middle class; racial quotas; and increasingly minute and unnecessary environmental regulation.

I say I grew into conservatism, but my nascent conservatism helped me to grow in the most important way: with regard to my faith. My mother always took me to church growing up, but it never felt like anything other than an obligation. I didn't begin to take it more seriously until I had my conservative awakening. This, too, I worked a little backward: Conservatives (many of them) were Christians, so what is it that Christians believed and how could it be defended in argument? Enter C. S. Lewis, the Christian apologist who answered exactly these questions. I learned about him in the pages of *National Review.* I read his *Mere Christianity,* a sturdy intellectual defense of Christianity. But Lewis's polemic somehow had a facile feel.

The Whittaker Chambers memoir *Witness* delved more deeply. It is a personal, wrenching explication of the struggle between good and evil inherent in the West's competition with the Soviet Union. The Foreword to the book is a famous "Letter to My Children" from Chambers. A passage in there struck me at the time: "Freedom is a need of the soul, and nothing else. It is in striving toward God that the soul strives continually after a condition of freedom. God alone is the inciter and guarantor of freedom. He is the only guarantor. External freedom is only an aspect of interior freedom. Political freedom, as the Western world has known it, is only a political reading of the Bible. Religion and freedom are indivisible. Without freedom the soul dies. Without the soul, there is no justification for freedom."

In his booming authorial voice, Chamber insists that God is to be taken seriously. *Witness* often reads like a Russian novel, and it was one of those that had the profoundest effect on me, *The Brothers Karamazov.* It wrestles with the problem of evil in unforgettable ways. The rationalist, rebellious brother Ivan refuses to take God's bargain of accepting the suffering of innocents as the price of the world working its way toward ultimate redemption. Ivan asks Alyosha, the faithful brother, if he would consent to a world where just one child has to be tortured, even if paradise ultimately awaits us. Alyosha's answer is utterly free of evasion: "No, I wouldn't consent."

Then, Alyosha adds, recalling Ivan's contention that no one can forgive innocent suffering, "There is a Being and He can forgive everything, all *and for all,* because He gave

His innocent blood for all and everything. You have forgotten Him, and on Him is built the edifice, and it is to Him they cry aloud, 'Thou art just, O Lord, for Thy ways are revealed!' " Alyosha's statement stuck. It took years and years to ripen—with prayer, scripture reading, and fellowship—but eventually it did, into a deep faith in Christ.

What does Christianity have to do with my conservatism? Nothing and everything.

Nothing, in the sense that it is perfectly possible to be a conservative without any such faith. Some of the highest-profile and most impressive conservative writers don't have a Christian faith, or any other. By the same token, obviously, liberals can be Christians. Personally, a deeper faith has made me more humble and a little less certain about my political beliefs, even if it hasn't changed any of my political beliefs per se.

Everything, in the sense that religious faith is the ultimate filial piety, the ultimate check on immanentizing the eschaton, the ultimate reality.

When I graduated from high school, I took my teenage conservatism to the University of Virginia, where I vented it—and slowly began to deepen and expand it—working on a conservative student publication called the *Virginia Advocate.* My heart jumped when I first discovered it existed, a tiny thing in a yellow cover stacked in the corners of a few university buildings. Writing for such a publication was what I had wanted most to do in college. It took me on a path that led—amazingly enough—to becoming the editor of *National Review.*

It would have stunned me to know in high school that I would get such an opportunity. That was a long time ago. But I occasionally recognize that high school kid in me, whenever I'm overzealous to win an argument or take pleasure in the sheer act of defending what seems difficult to defend. In my conservative journey, and journey as a person, I hope I'm always leaving that kid farther behind, even though—alas—there's no denying that it all started with him.

BIBLIOGRAPHY

Arendt, Hannah. *Eichmann in Jerusalem.* New York: Penguin Press, 1967.

Bartlett, Bruce R. *Impostor: How George W. Bush Bankrupted America and Betrayed the Reagan Legacy.* New York: Doubleday, 2006.

Bauer, Peter. *Dissent on Development.* Boston: Harvard University Press, 1972.

Berkowitz, Peter. *Nietzsche: The Ethics of an Immoralist.* Boston: Harvard University Press, 1995.

———. *Virtue and the Making of Modern Liberalism.* New Jersey: Princeton University Press, 1999.

Berns, Walter. *Freedom, Virtue & the First Amendment.* Westport, CT: Greenwood Publishing Group, 1969.

Bloom, Allan. *The Closing of the American Mind: How Higher Education Has Failed Democracy and Impoverished the Souls of Today's Students.* New York: Simon and Schuster, 1988.

Bowden, Mark. *Guests of the Ayatollah.* New York: Grove Atlantic, 2006.

Brooks, David. *Bobos in Paradise: The New Upper Class and How They Got There.* New York: Simon and Schuster, 2000.

———. *On Paradise Drive: How We Live Now (And Always Have) in the Future Tense.* New York: Simon and Schuster, 2004.

Buckley, William F. *Up from Liberalism.* Lanham, MD: Roman & Littlefield, 1991.

Burnham, James. *Machiavellians: Defenders of Freedom.* Washington, D.C.: Regnery Publishing, 1988.

———. *The Managerial Revolution: What Is Happening in the World.* Westport, CT: Greenwood Publishing Group, 1972.

———. *Suicide of the West.* New York: Crown Publishing Group, 1970.

Chambers, Whittaker. *Witness.* Washington, D.C.: Regnery Publishing, 1978.

Conquest, Robert. *The Great Terror: Stalin's Purge of the Thirties.* New York: Macmillan, 1973.

Crittenden, Danielle. *What Our Mothers Didn't Tell Us: Why Happiness Eludes the Modern Woman.* New York: Simon and Schuster, 1998.

Dallek, Robert. *Franklin D. Roosevelt and American Foreign Policy, 1932–1945.* New York: Oxford University Press, 1979.

Decter, Midge. *Liberal Parents, Radical Children.* New York: Coward, McCann & Geoghegan, 1975.

D'Souza, Dinesh. *The End of Racism: Principles for a Multiracial Society.* New York: Simon and Schuster, 1995.

———. *Illiberal Education: The Politics of Race and Sex on Campus.* New York: Free Press, 1990.

————. *Letters to a Young Conservative.* New York: Basic Books, 2001.

————. *What's So Great About America.* Washington, D.C.: Regnery Publishing, 2002.

Eberstadt, Mary. *Home-Alone America.* New York: Penguin Group, 2004.

Frank, Thomas. *What's the Matter with Kansas?: How Conservatives Won the Heart of America.* New York: Henry Holt & Company, 2004.

Fukuyama, Francis. *America at the Crossroads: Democracy, Power, and the Neoconservative Legacy.* New Haven, CT: Yale University Press, 2006.

Gilder, George. *Wealth and Poverty.* New York: Basic Books, 1980.

Goldwater, Barry. *The Conscience of a Conservative.* Victor Publishing Co., 1960.

Hazlitt, Henry. *Economics in One Lesson.* New York: Harper & Brothers, 1946.

Johnson, Paul. *Modern Times.* New York: HarperCollins, 1991.

Kirk, Russell. *The Conservative Mind: From Burke to Eliot.* Washington, D.C.: Regnery Publishing, 2001.

Kirkpatrick, Jeanne. *Dictatorships and Double Standards: Rationalism & Reason in Politics.* New York: Simon and Schuster, 1982.

Kristol, Irving. *Reflections of a Neoconservative.* New York: Basic Books, 1974.

Kurtz, Stanley. *All the Mothers Are One: Hindu India and the Cultural Reshaping of Psychoanalysis.* New York: Columbia University Press, 1992.

Lasch, Christopher. *The Culture of Narcissism.* New York: Warner Books, 1979.

Lévy, Bernard-Henri. *American Vertigo: Traveling America in the Footsteps of Tocqueville.* New York: Random House, 2006.

Lowry, Rich. *Legacy: Paying the Price for the Clinton Years.* Washington, D.C.: Regnery Publishing, 2003.

Mac Donald, Heather. *Are Cops Racist?* Chicago: Ivan Dee Publisher, 2003.

———. *The Burden of Bad Ideas: How Modern Intellectuals Misshape Our Society.* Chicago: Ivan Dee Publisher, 2000.

Moynihan, Daniel Patrick. "Defining Deviancy Down." *American Scholar,* Winter 1993.

Murray, Charles A. *Losing Ground: American Social Policy, 1950–1980.* New York: Basic Books, 1984.

Novak, Michael. *The Spirit of Democratic Capitalism,* Washington, D.C.: American Enterprise Institute, 2nd printing, 1982.

Orwell, Sonia and Angus, Ian, eds. *The Collected Essays, Journalism and Letters of George Orwell* (4 volumes). New York: Harcourt, Brace & Company, 1968.

Phillips, Kevin. *American Theocracy: The Peril and Politics of Radical Religion, Oil, and Borrowed Money in the 21st Century.* New York: Viking Press, 2006.

Podhoretz, Norman. *Breaking Ranks*. New York: Harper & Row, 1979.

———. *Making It*. New York: Random House, 1967.

———. *The Present Danger: Do We Have the Will to Reverse the Decline of American Power?* New York: Simon and Schuster, 1980.

———. *Why We Were in Vietnam*. New York: Simon and Schuster, 1982.

Rieff, Philip. *The Triumph of the Therapeutic*. New York: Harper & Row, 1968.

Satel, M.D., Sally. *PC, M.D.: How Political Correctness Is Corrupting Medicine*. New York: Basic Books, 2000.

Smith, Hedrick. *The Russians*. New York: Crown Publishing, 1976.

Unger, Roberto. *Knowledge and Politics*. New York: Free Press, 1975.

Wallis, Jim. *God's Politics: Why the Right Gets It Wrong and the Left Doesn't Get It*. San Francisco: HarperSanFrancisco, 2005.

Wolfe, Tom. *The Painted Word*. New York: Farrar Straus & Giroux, 1975.

Woolridge, Adrian and Mickelthwaite, John. *The Right Nation: Conservative Power in America*. London, England: Penguin Press, 2005.

ACKNOWLEDGMENTS

Thanks to Tad and Dianne Taube, the Taube Family Foundation, and John Raisian of the Hoover Institution for supporting this project; to literary agent Rafe Sagalyn and editors Mary Matalin and Kevin Smith of Simon and Schuster for believing in it; to Jeremy Rabkin for introducing me to Irving Kristol; to Irving Kristol for introducing me to journalism; and to P. J. O'Rourke, who first helped to kick around the idea for this book. Thanks also and as always to Frederick, Catherine, Isabel, and Alexandra for putting up with the domestic fallout of the writing hobby—and to Nick, for indulging it as he does everything else.

ABOUT THE EDITOR

MARY EBERSTADT is a Tad and Dianne Taube Foundation Fellow at the Hoover Institution, consulting editor to *Policy Review,* and author of *Home-Alone America* (Penguin/Sentinel, 2004). Her essays and reviews have been widely circulated. She has been managing editor of *The Public Interest,* executive editor of *The National Interest,* and was a speechwriter in the State Department during the Reagan administration.

Printed in the United States
By Bookmasters